PRAI

"A book t

siveness, ~~................,~~ and despair. This is not theory but real practices to generate peace through breathing, walking, connecting with community, emotional healing, and everything in between. If you are a fan of Thich Nhat Hanh and Martin Luther King Jr.'s nonviolent compassion in action — or if you are just tired of endless daily stress — let these inspiring stories and simple practices bring more peace and meaning to your soul."

— DAN RATHER, award–winning journalist and author of
What Unites Us

"Refreshingly simple, a lovely invitation. These monks inspire a sense of presence and possibility, whether hiking in nature or moving graciously through life."

— JACK KORNFIELD, author of *A Path with Heart*

"This beautiful book brings us home to the natural world of the wilds and the heart and mind. Clear like the sky, beautiful like this earth, the book and practices offered are a living treasure in our time."

— ROSHI JOAN HALIFAX, abbot of Upaya Zen Center and
author of *Standing at the Edge*

"Mindfulness as shared by these two monks is wilder than any episode of *Stranger Things*. Right from the first pages we glimpse the power, majesty, and excitement of living deeply in the present moment. Breathing in, I set the phone down and lace up my boots, and breathing out, I take a journey with the lineage of Thich Nhat Hanh, headed nowhere in particular except this present, wonderful moment — the sum of our life."

— DAVID HARBOUR, Tony Award–nominated actor

HIKING ZEN

ZEN

Train Your Mind in Nature

Brother Phap Xa
(Brother Equanimity)

Brother Phap Luu
(Brother Stream)

Foreword by Jon Kabat-Zinn

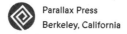

Parallax Press
Berkeley, California

Parallax Press
PO Box 7355
Berkeley, CA 94707
parallax.org

Parallax Press is the publishing division of Plum Village Community of
Engaged Buddhism, Inc.

Cover design by Katie Eberle
Text design by Maureen Forys, Happenstance Type-O-Rama
Cover artwork by Dave Yasenchak
Author photographs by Ramon Carreras Juanico

Printed in Canada by Marquis on FSC-certified paper

Parallax Press's authorized representative in the EU and EEA is SARL
Boutique La Bambouseraie Point UH, Le Pey, 24240 Thénac, France
Email: europe@parallax.org

Some of the names in this book have been changed to protect the privacy
of the participants on our hiking retreats.

Disclaimer: Please seek qualified advice to determine whether the
exercises in the book are suitable for you. Do not rely on this information
as a substitute for professional medical advice, diagnosis, or treatment.
The hiking tips and practices provided should not replace professional
guidance or personalized advice. Please consult with a qualified
professional before starting any new activity, particularly if you have
preexisting health conditions or concerns.

ISBN 978-0-984627-14-1
Ebook ISBN 978-0-984627-15-8

Library of Congress Control Number: 2024951652

2 3 4 5 6 MARQUIS 29 28 27 26 25

MIX
Paper | Supporting
responsible forestry
FSC® C103567

*To Thầy and all our ancestral
teachers, and to our parents
for their love and support*

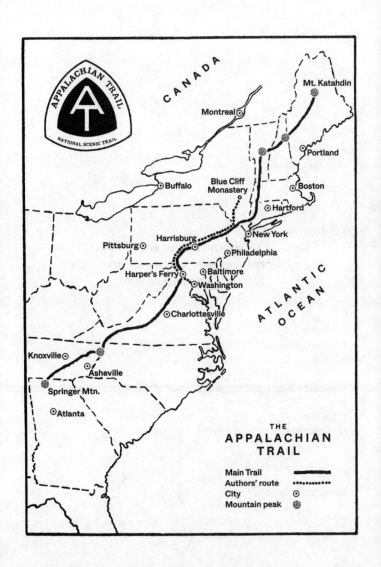

APPALACHIAN TRAIL

AT
NATIONAL SCENIC TRAIL

CANADA

Mt. Katahdin

Montreal

Portland

Buffalo

Blue Cliff
Monastery

Boston

Hartford

Pittsburg

Harrisburg

New York

Philadelphia

Harper's Ferry

Baltimore

Washington

A T L A N T I C

Charlottesville

O C E A N

Knoxville

Asheville

Springer Mtn.

Atlanta

THE
APPALACHIAN
TRAIL

Main Trail
Authors' route   •••••••••
City   ⊙
Mountain peak   ✳

CONTENTS

FOREWORD

The Buddha taught four foundational postures for formal meditation practice: sitting, standing, walking, and lying down. They are all different doors into the same room. "The room" is awareness itself—awareness of whatever is unfolding here and now, wherever you find yourself in your life in the present moment. The challenge of mindfulness is to learn to become, or better put, to *be* the knowing that awareness already is and always has been. This includes the knowing of what you don't know and may not even know you don't know. Sounds weird, I know, but there you have it.

But what I have just said, although true, is just a thought, merely a concept...unless you recognize that it may also be a portal—a portal to waking up to the present moment we call now and living life as if it really mattered in the only moment any of us ever has. That is what Zen is about. That is what this book is about. That is what mindfulness as both a formal meditation practice and as a way of being is about. They are all about you, about your deepest nature, and the quality and meaning in your life if you discover and learn to inhabit the boundless spaciousness of awareness in the present moment and to apprehend the interconnectedness of all things.

There is no place better to engage in such a practice than in nature itself, since we are never entirely out of nature. The air is nature, the sky is nature, the ground is nature, the wind is nature, the rain is nature, the snow is nature, the heat is nature, the cold, your body.... You are never out of nature and never far from your own truest nature, either.

Thus, the natural world can be a fantastic place to intimately observe the nature of your own mind, other people's minds, and your relationship to the surround, to the miracle of this analog world we have inherited from those who came before—ancestors going back and back and back who are, as the authors point out so evocatively, in some very real sense in us, a part of us, and more than merely genetically.

This book makes a powerful and enticing case for using the outer landscapes of nature to locate your own true nature and your place in the world, as well as to recognize the compelling need to listen deeply to, respect, and take care of Mother Earth at this moment of multiple planetary crises.

Hiking is an apt metaphor for how you might live your entire life as an adventure in being where you already are, wherever you find yourself, whatever the conditions, moment by moment by moment. As in life, the particular destination or goal you set in hiking is important. But it is equally important to allow yourself to be in the present moment and with each step, taking in what is unfolding—even if you are "behind schedule," even if the rain is dripping on your head and your clothes are soaking wet or someone has done something that triggers rage in you. Paying attention in this way, not only will you be refining your relationship with yourself, but equally with the natural world and with those you may be hiking with or wind up encountering along the trail.

The authors, Brother Phap Xa and Brother Phap Luu, are Westerners, disciples of the great Vietnamese Zen Master, Thich Nhat Hanh, who, with staggering determination and resolve, committed his entire life to waking up the world and to waging peace on multiple fronts, all undergirded by what he referred to as the miracle of mindfulness.

By virtue of their vows and their own meditation practice, these brothers know of what they speak, whether they are talking about Zen or about hiking. Having devoted their lives to this Dharma stream, relinquishing their secular identities, agendas, and possessions for the wandering monastic life—as did the original followers of the Buddha 2,600 years ago, giving rise to an unbroken lineage right up to the present—their voices convey an ease and authenticity that is both disarming and inspiring.

The reader may or may not wind up hiking with one or both of these Dharma teachers and guides at some point in the future, but you won't have to. As you read this book, you will find that you are already participating in a lovingly guided walk within a natural world that is happily still available to us. There are lots of wonderful lessons here, enough for a lifetime at least.

And who knows? Perhaps an opportunity has already arisen, or will arise down the road, for you to hike with one of the authors in person. And if not, at least you will have a better sense of the many ways you might cultivate greater mindfulness in nature and in everyday living, walking or hiking, whether on your own, with family, or in community, with this book in your pocket and maybe in your heart as well, as a trustworthy guide.

—JON KABAT-ZINN,
Northampton, Massachusetts,
January 17, 2025

The core hiking group of the seven-week Appalachian Trail mindful hiking retreat seated on the Jefferson Rock in Harpers Ferry, West Virginia, overlooking the Shenandoah River's confluence with the Potomac. From left to right: Brother Phap Khoi, Brother Phap Luu, Brother Phap Man, Brother Phap Xa, Ramon, and Brother Dao Hanh. (Photo credit: Tammy McCorkle)

INTRODUCTION

The Simple Act of Walking

Mindful walking is simple. You can do it right now, with one breath and one step. If you are alive and your legs are in good condition, you have everything you need.

Mindful walking is difficult. Forces beyond our control drive us to hurry, and we stumble over ourselves—in our work and in our relationships—as one day rushes into the next. Where are we going? Will we know once we get there? Will we stop running before we die?

Mindful walking is the foundation of hiking Zen. Training yourself to stop this hell-bent sprint through life, to look deeply and see the profound beauty of the present moment, is one of the most difficult—and yet most rewarding—things we can do. Hiking Zen is mindful walking *in nature*, and it can be one of the most fulfilling ways to make this change. Stopping your habit of hurrying—turning off the music, the news, or the podcast—and opening yourself to the forest, the stream, the mountain, the prairie, the desert (or even to the daisy pushing through a crack in the pavement) can deeply alter your experience of the world and yourself within it.

Often in everyday life, we walk to arrive somewhere. Hiking Zen's most basic principle is to arrive in each step we take, to stop losing ourselves in thoughts about the past or future. Like walking meditation, hiking Zen is not an exercise, but a joy. We walk not to arrive anywhere or to attain anything — we walk just to enjoy walking. We train our mind to stay in the present moment. In doing so, we allow this moment to be a moment of happiness.

The simplicity of mindful walking belies its transformative power. Putting one foot in front of the other, an act as fundamental as it is overlooked, is central to a journey of mindfulness that supports personal and collective liberation. When we experience stability and wisdom in our bodies, we are not swept away by strong emotions like anger or despair, and we can respond skillfully to the big existential crises confronting our society and planet today — climate change, political turmoil, and everyday violence.

But weaving Zen practices into time spent outdoors is more than a self-care practice, more than an exercise that bolsters our ability to remain engaged in difficult times. It is certainly not a means to an end. Slowing down, synchronizing our steps with the rhythms of our breath, and recognizing *interbeing* — our connection with everything within and around us — at an embodied, cellular level is simply a profound experience. Life-changing.

This is the path we have walked as two Zen monks following the Plum Village tradition of Engaged Buddhism for the last two decades. "Zen" comes from the Sanskrit root word *dhyāna*, which simply means "meditation." Engaged Buddhism is a movement started in Vietnam by our teacher, Zen Master Thich Nhat Hanh, and others, to make Buddhist practices relevant to our times — responsive to violence, poverty, and social injustice. He and his colleagues worked for peace amid the suffering brought about by French colonialism and subsequently, the war between communist-backed and American-backed forces in his country in the 1960s and '70s. Thich Nhat Hanh, or as we call him, "Thay" (a Vietnamese word of respect usually translated as "teacher," pronounced like the English word "tie") founded the Plum Village tradition after being exiled from Vietnam for his peace work. From the beginning, the Plum Village tradition has been rooted in a commitment to bring the compassion and clarity cultivated on the meditation cushion into the world—to tend to suffering and injustice at every level. Personal transformation is intimately linked with action. Developing a deep awareness of our bodies and our connection with nature with mindful walking is an essential practice in our lineage.

As monks who hike and who offer Hiking Zen retreats, we love to be outside. We love to feel the earth under our feet. Mindful hiking has brought both of us profound healing and peace, as we will share in these pages, and we want to make this transformative, deceptively simple activity available to as many people as possible.

Most wisdom traditions (and Zen is no exception) offer periods of retreat as prolonged opportunities to deepen one's practice, stability, and open-heartedness with the support of community. When we refer to "Zen practice," "the practice," or "our practice," we are talking about the aspects of daily behavior—from breathing to sitting, walking, eating, even brushing our teeth—that strengthen mindful, peaceful, compassionate awareness and action. Such retreats often happen in meditation centers, with participants arriving for days or weeks to follow a shared schedule of practice and reflection. Hiking Zen retreats take this program into more wild spaces. People arrive bearing backpacks, tents, raincoats, and pots and pans, and together we take our practice onto the trail, into nature.

Being in Nature

Nature is everywhere. Our bodies are made from plants, sun, and water; weeds grow in bits of unused land scattered through every town; even our machines and infrastructure—steel, concrete, plastic—are made of elements taken from the earth. *Artificial* and *natural* are just concepts we create. This book, however, focuses on experiences in the undeveloped natural habitats that have nurtured us and been integral to our development as a species on this planet.

For those new to practicing it, mindfulness immersion and movement in the wild—being in unstructured nature—is extremely beneficial. There remains something special about the spaciousness of being outside for hours, days, or even weeks at a time in a landscape less impacted by human intervention. Being under the open sky, surrounded by trees or other plants, brings us unique possibilities of connection and exploration into our human experience—both our difficulties and our healing.

Being mindful of our bodies and our interconnectedness with the earth can offer a stark contrast to our experience in the urban environments in which many of us reside. In cities, which bustle with distractions and relentless sensory stimuli, it is not easy to remain centered. With the Internet more and more accessible, even when we leave the city behind, we bring the noise of advertising, consumerism, entertainment, social media, and news along with us.

Out there, in the forest, the prairie, the desert, or on the hillside, is the unknown. Because of our modern way of living, we may well have forgotten what to do and how to behave outside. The unknown can be scary. It may feel more comfortable to live indoors in a house or to drive to work in a car. Observe, though, how the boxes we spend so much time in affect our minds. The mind mirrors its habitat. If we aren't careful, our worldview is drawn with very clear borders: this is mine, that is yours—we become territorial, overly attached to our boxes. Unused to spending extended time outside, we can still feel some resistance, some sense of separation or fear that keeps us from deep immersion. Through embodied mindfulness, we remember the richness of quiet presence that is possible amid the sounds of nature.

Make no mistake; it takes courage to temporarily cut off our electronic connection to the world. But when we do it, immersion in nature can help us to truly connect to our wholeness, our stability, and to a sense of awe that enables us to take care of our anxiety, depression, and fear. Taking time to be with what is within us and around us, supported by the ground beneath our feet and the sky above our heads, we find a respite from modern chaos—a place where we can uncouple from fast-paced urban life and transform our ways of being and thinking. We find space to calm our minds, reacquaint ourselves with our bodies, and cultivate a deeper awareness of our thoughts and emotions.

Practicing mindfulness in nature is deeply rooted in Zen. The Buddha had a habit of meditating outdoors and invited students to come out from their "dusty and crowded houses" when they became monks and nuns. These early practitioners learned to live outside, in harmony with the changing seasons, close to the elements.

But the Buddha wasn't encouraging his students to leave their homes to learn to be good campers. As we deepen our understanding of nature, we meet our mind and our emotions. We see deep truths that free us. Observing nature, we realize everything changes, and our habitual fear begins to loosen its grip. To train our mind with the support of the earth from which we come is to experience lasting transformation. Even if, from an early age, you didn't have access to the outdoors, you can start now.

To claim our sovereign nature as free, wild, endlessly creative, and beautiful creatures, we need to train ourselves *by untraining ourselves*. We need to step out of the boxes in which we find ourselves and unravel our contemporary conditioning. Only then can we move from compulsion to conscience, building a stable foundation for both personal and planetary well-being.

How to Use
This Book

Please see this book as notes from spiritual friends on the path. It is an invitation for all of us to clear the brushwood from our minds and rediscover an old path that is already there — a path leading to our true nature, to freedom on Earth, our home.

The book in your hands invites radical change from within. These pages explore questions people often bring to our retreats:

How can I experience more joy and peace?

What is my place in the world?

How can I skillfully engage with the many challenges plaguing our planet without burning out?

Our own transformation and the transformation we have witnessed in others when we slow down on the trail and reconnect with what is beneath, around, and within all of us are the bones of this book. In the following chapters, the two of us trace the roots of our monastic paths, share our experiences leading dozens of Zen retreats in nature, and offer concrete practices to cultivate wholeness and healing. We share journal entries and personal reflections, drawing particularly on a seven-week Hiking Zen retreat on the legendary Appalachian Trail, a 2,200-mile walking route from Georgia to Maine. Our path started in Blue Cliff Monastery's backyard in upstate New York and ended forty-two days later at the National Mall in Washington, DC, where we sat together in meditation.

At times throughout the book, we refer to a bell. From time to time during our retreats we invite everyone, as they listen to the sound of a bell, to stop what they're doing and come back to the present-moment experience of their breathing. In the Plum Village tradition, a bell used in this way is called a *mindfulness bell*. But you don't need to already have a mindfulness practice to enjoy this book. Everything you need to start is here. Each chapter has specific practices to help you explore mindful hiking on your own or with your community as well as suggestions for applying the practices in your daily life.

We hope you slip this book into your backpack, bag, or back pocket the next time you head out your door. Ultimately, we encourage you to explore your own experience in nature. Zen is very clear about this: take what is offered and then see for yourself. Give the practices time and notice their impact. Adapt what doesn't work for you. As we say in Zen, do not confuse the finger pointing at the moon with the moon itself. Your engagement and direct experience are required.

We hope this book is a call to a deeper understanding of ourselves, our place in the world as human beings, and our relationship with all that surrounds and supports us, for the benefit of all beings.

Happy trails!

CHAPTER ONE
Breath of Life

Snowy Morning on the Shawangunk Ridge Trail

PHAP LUU

I stick my head out from my camping hammock to behold the forest blanketed in soft morning snow, gentle flakes continuing to drift down. The air temperature hovers just above freezing—not too cold to think of getting up for a hot breakfast. I swing my feet around and step into my hiking boots—tied loosely so I can slip them on and off while in camp—taking care not to touch the snow with my woolen socks.

The sun rises behind a thick blanket of clouds. It's the second day of our seven-week Hiking Zen retreat. I hear the faint stirrings of other walkers: fellow guide Ramon in his hammock, monk Brother Dao Hanh in his, and hikers rustling out of their tents. A group of some fifteen of us—brown-robed monks and laypeople—silently gather around the clear sound of the bell resonating across a mat of snow and through naked spring tree trunks. Morning meditation: for thirty minutes, we sit in silence—some on fallen logs, others with legs crossed on thermal mats, many with sleeping bags wrapped about them. The crystalline tinkle of snowflakes falling on the forest floor penetrates the quiet.

Sitting still with legs crossed, I notice my breath moving in and out of my body. After a few minutes, I turn my attention to the water nature within me—the blood coursing through my veins, the saliva warm in my mouth, what is left in my bladder of the urine I released a few minutes ago next to a tree beside my hammock. The snowflakes around me bear the same water nature, having evaporated off the surface of oceans and lakes to gather as clouds—uncountable droplets that, in this cold weather, have become snow. Already the flakes transform back into water and drip down to saturate the dead leaves piled on the still-warm earth.

Another bell, and the meditation ends. The silence continues with warm smiles as the prospect of breakfast brings us to our feet. Ramon begins cooking oats as I head off with empty bottles and a water filter toward the gurgling sounds to the south. A glance at the curve of the valley is enough to spot the low point that would naturally funnel the waters into a stream. I follow the stream uphill until I find a spring pulsing up out of the ground. Crouching on my haunches, I unwind the filter's tube and slip it into the cold fountain. The warm pulse of my blood meets the cool pulse of groundwater emerging from the earth as, with rhythmic movements of my arm, I draw the flow through the tube and watch filtered water spill into the bottle.

"Water comes from high mountain sources, water comes from deep in the earth, miraculously water comes to me and sustains all life"—the words of the Zen poem (or *gatha*) that I learned to recite as a novice whenever I turned on a faucet comes to mind. Dozens of such gathas invite us to become aware of the mundane and not-so-mundane moments of our lives. Part of one's monastic training is to practice with these gathas throughout the day; they become integrated in everything we do. Here in

HIKING ZEN

the forest, the wisdom of the gatha seems evident—how could anyone take for granted the miracle of water once they experience how crystallized clouds now wet as snow seep into humus and recharge a pulsing spring so it can flow into a bottle for us to drink?

A silent breakfast done, smiles and joyful laughter follow. On Hiking Zen retreats, we practice mindfulness 24/7, not only during seated or walking meditation. Now we pack up our gear mindfully, feeling the texture of different fabrics in our hands and noticing the rise and fall of our breaths. Before heading out, we come together in a circle and as is common on these retreats, read aloud from *Touching the Earth*, a collection of deeply reverent texts Thay wrote. These short meditative passages help us remember to connect to the Earth, our emotions, our ancestors, and all of nature, in and around us, in the very way we walk. Today, I read:

> *I vow to walk as someone who is free and awake. I vow that in every step I take my feet will truly touch the earth, and I will be aware I am walking on the ground of reality and not in a dream. Walking like that, I am in touch with everything that is wonderful and miraculous in the universe. I vow to walk in such a way that my feet will impress on the earth the seal of freedom and peace. I know steps taken like this have the capacity to heal my body and mind as well as the planet Earth itself.*

Then, mindful of our breathing and the touch of our feet upon the earth—the first slippery steps of the morning will require special concentration—we set off along the mossy trail, listening to the melting snow.

On Breathing

Mindfulness means being present to the beauty within and around us. If we get lost in our thinking when we walk in nature, we're not present for the wonders around us. There are many flowers, but we do not see them. The birds sing, but we do not hear them. Breathing is the anchor that keeps us from drifting away on the current of our thoughts when we walk. When we are conscious of our breathing throughout the day, our capacity to be mindful grows stronger, and we find we're able again to come back to, recognize, and enjoy the many wondrous things alive in the present moment.

We all breathe all day long, otherwise we couldn't live. Breathing is something natural; our body takes care of it. When we bring our mind back to our body and our breath within it, it's very natural to feel peaceful. When we say an affirmation such as "peace is the breathing," we can ask ourselves: Is it true? Do I feel peaceful when I breathe in and out?

If we don't naturally feel peaceful when we breathe, we may be preoccupied by thoughts that stop us from being fully present. As human beings, we tend to let our thoughts run in circles, endlessly dragging us into the past or pulling us away into the future. This kind of compulsive thinking can be a prison. But when we allow the present to unfold with awareness, we're able to feel gratitude for our healthy feet. Gratitude that we can walk upright on this beautiful planet earth! Our eyes can be in touch with the wondrous world around us — white clouds, fresh streams of water, colorful meadows. We realize we can always do something to nourish our happiness, that we already have all we need to be happy. We train our minds to transform our anxiety and depression into happiness.

When the mind is scattered, it's difficult to concentrate on anything. Our mind is like a monkey eating a mango in the tree but already looking at another mango, unable to really taste the one in its mouth. When this happens, we must first recognize our monkey mind without judging. Simply notice, "Oh, I'm really caught in thinking right now" and return to your somatic experience—the feeling in your body—of your breath. If it feels easier, you may like to experiment with tuning your attention to the sounds around you or the sensations in your body rather than the internal experience of breath—just be careful to pick a solid anchor for your attention and then give yourself time to settle into the practice. Restlessly switching from one anchor to another won't help.

Imagination can play a central role in a healthy, happy life. Countless experiences documented in poems, novels, movies, and other art forms are a testament to the power of imagination. The make-believe world in our minds can give us insight into our lives and the world around us. Yet when we develop a habit of getting distracted by and caught in our imagination, we create a separation between our body and mind and miss a precious opportunity to understand the very real sources of our pain and hurt. Mindfulness can help us choose to stop getting pulled away by our imagination when the more skillful and appropriate response to a painful situation is *present moment awareness of what is going on within and around us*.

So often, we look for something to occupy our mind. We look for something to do. We work, study, or find entertainment. We don't want to face ourselves. What are we running from? What are we afraid of? In our modern world, restlessness is a major obstacle to contentment and happiness. When you notice agitation, find an anchor in your breath, in your embodied awareness of the present moment. Our experience on each hiking retreat has been that our mind does naturally calm down; it just takes a little time and patience. There is no need to run. There has never been a need to run.

PRACTICE
Mindful Breathing

We have often heard the sentence, "Don't just sit there, do something." Thay liked to turn it around and say, "Don't just do something, sit there."

Practicing mindful breathing can establish a foundation for transformation. On our mindful hiking retreats, mindful breathing is the first practice we teach. It is basic but powerful and can enrich your day-to-day experience. Mindful breathing can be done in a seated position, traditionally on the ground with legs crossed or in a lotus position, but you can also practice it while walking, standing, or lying down. You may like to sit at the foot of a tree, on a rock, or sling a hammock and enjoy breathing as you lie in it. Anywhere is fine.

When we practice mindful breathing in a seated position, we first establish a stable posture, upright and relaxed. Imagine a thread passing through your spine, reaching from its base up through the crown of your head, and someone gently pulling up on the thread. Let your shoulders relax and hang off this imaginary thread. Your eyes may be open, closed, or half-open, gazing softly at the ground. While practicing mindful breathing, we do not control the breath or have any expectations of how the breathing should happen. We follow the natural flow of the breath. We don't think about the breath; we feel the breath directly in our body, from the inside.

So we don't get lost in our thoughts, we may listen to a guided meditation with keywords to help us remain present in the moment. For example, you can read the guided meditation below and breathe gently in sync with the words. Don't worry if your breath doesn't fully align with the length of the lines; don't try to control your breath. Just keep coming back to your experience of breath in your body and an awareness of being alive.

> *Breathing in, I know I am breathing in.*
>
> *Breathing out, I know I am breathing out.*
>
> > *In.*
> > *Out.*
>
> *Breathing in, I follow the entire length of my in-breath, from the beginning to the end, with all my attention. I am aware of the air entering my nostrils, moving down through my throat, and filling my lungs, my chest and belly rising.*
>
> *Breathing out, I follow with all my attention the entire length of my out-breath: my belly falling as the air moves up and out through my mouth and nostrils.*
>
> > *Following the in-breath.*
> > *Following the out-breath.*

Breathing in, I am aware of my whole body. I experience my body just as it is, free from ideas or expectations about how I may wish it to be.

Breathing out, I smile to my body, accepting it just as it is.

> *In, aware of my whole body.*
> *Out, smiling to my body.*

Breathing in, I relax my body.

Breathing out, I release any tension in my body. I shine the light of mindfulness on any place in my body where there are knots or tension, and I feel that tension becoming looser and unraveling.

> *In, relaxing the body.*
> *Out, releasing tension.*

Breathing in, I feel joy to be alive in the present moment.

Breathing out, I smile to the wonders of life, within me and around me.

> *In, joy to be alive.*
> *Out, smiling to life.*

Breathing in, I see I have more than enough conditions to be happy, right here and right now.

Breathing out, I have nowhere to go and nothing to do.

> *In, conditions to be happy.*
> *Out, nowhere to go, nothing to do.*

After reading through the meditation and following the guided breathing, allow yourself to fully relax and observe several breaths without words, perhaps enjoying a moment of silence.

Bringing It Home

Mindful breathing is a practice that can be built into your day—whether right after waking up in the morning, during the day when you'd like to relax, or before you go to sleep. It's best to practice in the sitting position, but you may also like to try while lying in bed. Notice your breath coming in and out, your belly rising and falling, and move through the first few steps above to cultivate embodied attention and joy in the present moment. Even just following one of these steps for twenty to thirty seconds can transform a moment of stress into one of peace.

A short, simple practice to bring joy to your mind when you wake is to sit up in bed for a few moments before you rise and recite the following gatha silently while noticing the sensations of your breath:

Waking up this morning, I smile
Twenty-four brand new hours are before me
I vow to live fully each moment
And to look at all beings with eyes of compassion.[1]

CHAPTER TWO

Mindful Walking

The Spiritual Path and the Appalachian Trail

PHAP LUU

In my early twenties before becoming a monk, I hiked the Appalachian Trail section from Bull's Bridge, Connecticut, to Mount Washington in New Hampshire. I had been living in the New Haven Zen Center, and I began from there with the idea of ending up at Maple Forest Monastery,* a Plum Village practice center I had discovered the year before. As I made my way along the summit of Bromley Mountain in Vermont, I met another

---

* Note on locations of places in the book: Plum Village Monastery, where both of us ordained as novices and became Dharma teachers, is located in the Dordogne, two hours east of Bordeaux, France. Blue Cliff Monastery, where we started the seven-week Appalachian Trail hike and where Brother Phap Xa was a resident monk from 2007 until 2010, is in upstate New York near Newburgh. Deer Park Monastery, where Brother Phap Luu has lived in alternation with Plum Village since 2004 and where he regularly leads mindful backpacking retreats, is in San Diego County in California. Brother Phap Xa has lived at the European Institute of Applied Buddhism since 2010, where he leads mindful walking retreats in nature numerous times each year. Maple Forest Monastery, the first Plum Village monastery in the US, opened in 1997 and then closed and moved to Blue Cliff Monastery in 2007.

young man. Strawberry, as he was called, had been hiking solo since his hiking partner, whom he had met on the trail, had become injured. As often happens when you meet someone on a long-distance hike, Strawberry and I fell into step together. An athletic, curly-haired young duck hunter and high-school football star from Tennessee with piercing blue eyes, Strawberry was taking time on the trail to reflect on whether to pursue missionary work in Central America. He was, it turned out, an evangelical Christian. Soon, though, he began asking an unending stream of questions about Buddhism.

At the time, I was something of an evangelical Buddhist, so we were well matched. Friends and family could scarcely get near me without getting an earful of Buddhist teachings. It felt like a stroke of luck to meet Strawberry in the high woods of Vermont. Here, we could have the friendly showdown that typified the struggles in the collective American consciousness of young spiritual men at the time: Which was better, what I perceived as the more sensible and yet deeply spiritual path of Zen or the faith-based, literalist interpretation of biblical Christianity?

Strawberry proved an affable and curious conversation partner. Our talks continued over a few days as we walked under the soft white pines that flanked the trail through the Green Mountains, taking breaks to munch on energy bars and bananas mixed with wild sorrel I gathered from the undergrowth. Strawberry had been trucking along at a thirty-mile-a-day pace. His legs were hardened and toned by the more than 1,660 miles he had covered in the previous two months. He called himself a purist—he accepted no excuse for missing walking even one yard of the official trail, as strictly defined by the Appalachian Trail Conservancy.

Keeping up with Strawberry was grueling yet exhilarating. As he peppered me with questions about Buddhism—always from a place of tolerance, safely grounded in his own rock-solid Christian faith—he repeated his favorite phrase, a sort of koan (a type of question or riddle often used in Zen to pierce through our attachment to intellect) he considered in every situation: "WWMTD?" "What would Mother Theresa do?" I don't know how many times he told me: "In any situation, any problem, ask yourself: WWMTD? What would Mother Theresa do?" It was a novel approach for me; immediately, I shifted one letter to make my own question: WWTBD—What would the Buddha do?

Strawberry regaled me with stories of training his beagles for duck hunting and leading tourist hunting parties through the swamps of Tennessee. Although he was modest, I could tell he was admired and had prowess as a quarterback on his football team and that he had become something of a local celebrity when he set out to thru-hike the Appalachian Trail, receiving donations of support along the way. In some ways, he was a wandering mendicant of old, but with a thoroughly contemporary American appearance.

Throughout our rambling conversations, he returned repeatedly, with a curiosity that surprised him, to ask me about Zen. I spoke about having recently become vegetarian, a choice rooted in the deeper vow Buddhists take to save all sentient beings from suffering. Strawberry received my thoughts with humility and a genuine interest, making me wonder at the openness of such a young, avowed evangelical likely on his way to missionary work.

After two nights, we had covered fifty miles. I was unaware of the pounding toll on my body—partly because I had placed all my attention on our stimulating conversation and partly due to the discipline I had developed as a long-distance runner. The next day, however, I could no longer ignore a nagging pain in my knee. Sixty miles in around forty-eight hours was too big a jump for my body, which had been happily pushing fifteen- to twenty-mile days. I told Strawberry and his trail partner, who had shown up again after attending to his own injury, that I needed to rest. I laid myself out on a sleeping pad beside the trail in the waning afternoon light, and they went on.

We never saw each other again.

The next few days, I looked eagerly for Strawberry's mark in the hiking registers, sometimes catching his name next to the drawn figure of a strawberry. Now, over two decades on, I wonder where his path has taken him. As for me, the hiking retreats I participate in today are very different from that hike and other solo hikes I took as a young man. Now, I don't so much talk about Zen as live it, in community. Along with others, I organize hiking retreats where we practice awakening into freedom as we walk: we take care of the whole group, leave no one behind, and walk mindfully enough to avoid injury. But the same sense of inquisitive friendship and passionate life purpose runs through me still.

A Path of Happiness

PHAP XA

I've enjoyed Zen hiking retreats for many years. In 2010, seven years after I became a monk, I moved to the European Institute of Applied Buddhism (EIAB) in Germany, where I still live. Hiking retreats were already a popular tradition when I arrived. Like other courses we offer on themes such as dealing with emotions or taking care of stress, mindful walking retreats in nature focus on applying Zen teachings to daily life.

The abundant hiking trails around our center make the EIAB an ideal place for staging hiking retreats. Sister Kaira Jewel[2] — an American nun who has since left her monastic robes behind to become a lay Dharma teacher—started leading these hiking retreats in 2009 with two German friends, Johannes and Ivo, who led us on beautiful paths through forests and fields. Johannes was a forest ranger in the area and always happy to share his experience and knowledge about the surrounding land. We hardly ever walked on asphalt.

In these woods, I learned to combine two of my passions: meditation and hiking. Meditative or mindful walking is not something new, though it was truly revelatory for me. Walking meditation, bringing wholehearted presence to each step, is at the very core of most schools of Zen practice, and in our own Plum Village tradition, it is part of our daily life—not just a formal practice we explore in the meditation hall, but something we do as a community while we move about throughout the day.

Our hiking retreats, though, tend to happen at a higher speed of walking, and they happen in nature. We're out in the elements, at first just for one day, carrying everything we need—water, food for lunch, layers—in our backpacks. We walk mindfully in silence with opportunities to converse during breaks.

Typically, these original day hikes were around ten miles long, we hiked at a moderate pace, and we took many breaks for rest and reflection. We began with morning sitting meditation and breakfast at the institute, packed our lunches, and then started walking around 9:00 a.m. We'd walk and rest all day before returning to the institute for dinner and a sharing circle to listen to whatever each hiker wanted to say about their experience.

I am always happy to hear when hiking retreats have a long-term impact. For example, a woman from the Netherlands recently told me that after she returned home from one of our hiking retreats, she made the commitment to enjoy walking the five miles to her workplace each day. Another regular participant, a retired Dutchman around seventy years old, also now walks several hours daily. Hiking and walking, done with mindfulness, can bring joy and peace to our days.

Sister Jewel left the EIAB in 2013, and I began to lead our hiking retreats, eventually seeking new routes—a very enjoyable pursuit. The hiking retreats became increasingly popular; we went from two to six a year. Clearly, the simple act of walking in nature met a need. Now, in summertime, we offer a shorter retreat with less hiking and more unstructured time dwelling in nature; participants are invited to bring their own hammock and make themselves comfortable in the forest. This retreat has proven very popular.

In 2014, our teacher, Thay, suffered a stroke. That autumn, our whole community in Germany (around fifty monks and nuns) traveled to our main practice center, Plum Village, in France, to visit him. It was a precious moment for me to return to my root temple, the place I had been ordained at as a novice monk; even after living in other centers for seven years, I still felt deeply at home in Plum Village. We arrived in the dark around midnight, but I could see the silhouettes of the high pine trees Thay himself had planted in the early eighties. I heard the wind chimes near the dining hall and, looking up, was again in awe of the especially bright stars in the night sky. Remote from city lights and constant traffic, I sensed the same peace I had experienced years earlier.

One day while I was in Plum Village, I went on a walk with brother Phap Luu, who lived there at the time. While we walked, I shared my thoughts about the hiking retreats I'd been leading, which had continued in much the same way as when Sister Jewel had led them. "People are happy, so why change things?" I wondered. But, at the same time, I had a dream, and it felt like the right time to share it: "A kind of backpacking retreat," I told my monastic brother, "where we're out in nature 24/7. We would eat, drink, sleep, and meditate on our way, maybe for a week or longer. No base camp."

It was no accident I chose this moment with this person to voice my hope. In our community, I couldn't think of a person more likely to embrace this idea than Phap Luu—I knew he'd backpacked for several weeks on the Appalachian Trail before ordaining. As our conversation continued, I could tell walking that trail again on a meditation retreat appealed to him. And when Phap Luu is fired up about something, it's likely to become reality.

On Walking

Birds may fly and fish may live their whole lives underwater, but the real miracle for human beings—as Zen Master Linji taught—is to walk on the Earth. Evolutionary science confirms his insight. Our feet, heels, toes, Achilles tendons, buttocks, waists, necks, inner ear, and eye reflexes all uniquely and specifically evolved so we could walk and run upright on the African savannah.[3] This is a true miracle. And yet, every day we take this miracle for granted.

Our practice is to arrive in each step on the path and to enjoy it. To enjoy our steps, we first need to be aware of them. However obvious this sounds, it's easier said than done. We usually think about the past or plan for the future while we walk; we're not fully present for our steps, fully present in our feet and in our bodies. We don't fully enjoy our steps. We can't be free unless we're free from regrets about the past, worries about the future, and strong emotions in the present.

When we practice hiking Zen, we walk in nature and we are, at the same time, on a spiritual path. At the end of the hike, we may be somewhere else, so we can say this is our destination, but if we only think about the destination, we lose touch with the many wonders present within and around us each moment of our walk. Enjoying our steps while walking is a habit we cultivate, not something that comes out of nowhere. We create this habit by watering seeds of happiness and attentiveness inside ourselves and by intentionally choosing circumstances in which we can enjoy walking.

There are many seeds in our minds. Our hearts and our minds are like gardens, each full of beautiful flowers and beautiful seeds—the potential for happiness, generosity, kindness, and love. Everything needs nourishment, though—some kind of food—to survive. Plants and flowers grow when they receive water, soil, sunshine, and air. In the same way, our happiness blooms when it is nourished by regularly taking the time for a walk, enjoying a cup of tea with a good friend, or taking in a beautiful sunset, for example. Without nourishment, nothing lasts long.

It's an art to be happy; it's also an art, when we have some kind of pain, to learn how to recognize it and take care of it. To walk on the path of happiness we must be able to take care of our suffering. Taking care of suffering is taking care of happiness.

Step out into any street in any city in the world and observe people walking. It won't be long before you see people multitasking, talking on their phones, eating food, in a hurry to arrive at their destination. This is our collective tendency: we walk with a destination in mind, and we try to do as much as possible along the way. Our walk is a means to an end. Even when we focus on the act of walking, our attention may be distracted by measuring ourselves against a future goal with a watch that counts our steps or our calories burned and measures our heart rate or the distance we cover.

In the monastery there's only one style of walking: walking meditation. As monks, we practice taking mindful steps whenever we're walking. When we practice it inside the meditation hall, we go very slowly. We take one step during the in-breath and one step during the out-breath. We don't talk as we walk. This allows us to be mindful, to be fully present for ourselves and our surroundings.

But walking meditation can be practiced outside as well as inside. Thay's experience of the powerful nourishment and healing of mindful steps taken outside, in touch with nature, inspired him. He brought the traditional practice of walking meditation out of the meditation hall and into the natural world—a revolutionary act for East Asian Buddhists.

Mindfulness has no set speed. On our hiking retreats, we practice walking at a pace that allows us to retain our mindfulness. Our speed may be like that of others on the trail, but our way of walking is mindful and at ease. With each step, we come back to the present moment by bringing all our attention to our breathing and our steps. When we keep our mind one hundred percent on our breathing and our steps, amazingly, our thoughts about the past and the future disappear. Our anxieties and even some deep-rooted troubles recede. We become fully present to the wonders of life in the here and now.

Being able to keep our presence of mind like this nourishes our whole selves and brings healing. If we notice our mind racing, we can accept this without judgment and simply return to our mindful walk. Do I feel joy as I walk? We can also ask ourselves:

> Am I happy when I walk?
>
> Do I walk as a free person without projects, without somewhere to go?
>
> Am I hurrying?
>
> Am I enjoying my steps?

We can train ourselves to walk as free people, not chained to our goals or a destination. We can practice arriving in every step, in the here and now. We can learn to touch peace and happiness in each step. We don't have to look for peace and happiness in a faraway future.

PRACTICE

Bringing Our Breaths and Steps Together

Here is a practice you can do to come back to the present moment by coordinating your breathing and your steps. To start, stand stably on the Earth; feel the ground beneath your feet; establish a connection with the Earth and your breathing. You may like to put your hands on your belly to feel it rising and falling with your breath.

In walking meditation, we coordinate our breathing with our steps in a natural way, without forcing the breathing or the steps. When you master this, you can practice mindful walking at any pace. To start, though, it is helpful to walk slowly. For example, we may practice taking one breath with each step while focusing on being in our bodies. Repeat the following phrases silently to yourself as you walk:

Breathing in, I step with my left foot. Breathing out, I step with my right foot.

In, left / Out, right.

Breathing in, I'm aware of the contact the sole of my left foot makes with the ground. Breathing out, I'm aware of the contact the sole of my right foot makes with the ground.

In, left / Out, right.

Breathing in, I arrive fully with my left step. Breathing out, I feel at home with my right step.

In, arrived / Out, at home.

Breathing in, I'm fully present right here with my left step. Breathing out, I'm fully present in the now with my right step.

In, here / Out, now.

Walking at a natural, relaxed pace, you may experiment with taking two or three steps with each in-breath and three or four steps with each out-breath. Your out-breath may be longer than your in-breath. If it is natural for the in- and out-breath to be the same length, you may find you take the same number of steps for each. There's no need to change the rhythm of your breathing or your steps; just notice naturally how many steps you take with each in-breath and how many steps you take with each out-breath. As you find yourself walking up and down hills, the number of steps per breath may change. That's fine! The important thing is to keep your attention on your breath and your step. We arrive at home in the here and the now with each step.

We can first coordinate our breathing with our steps and then introduce rhythmic keywords to help us stay in the present moment. These words aren't for you to repeat mindlessly, but for you to practice with, to support you to truly arrive with each step, be at home in each step. The keywords can help you to focus your mind in the present moment, wherever you're walking.

Breathing in, I take two or three steps. Breathing out, I take three or four steps.

In, in / Out, out, out.

Breathing in, with each step I arrive in the present moment. Breathing out, with each step I feel at home.

Arrived, arrived / At home, at home, at home.

Breathing in, with each step I am truly here walking on Mother Earth. Breathing out, with each step there is only now.

Here, here / Now / now / now.

Breathing in, I dwell in the present moment. Breathing out, this is a wonderful moment. I am surrounded by the wonders of life.

Present moment / Wonderful moment.

You can take any element of the practice offered here and engage with it for the whole of the walking meditation, whether indoors or in nature. For example, you could set a timer and walk for twenty minutes, gently guiding yourself with the keywords "arrived" on the in-breath and "at home" on the out-breath the entire time. These phrases help you bring attention to your feet as they touch the ground and your breath whenever your focus wanders. If you find the keywords don't match the rhythm of your steps, feel free to adjust them.

Explore this practice for yourself, and notice whether, over time, it helps you to free yourself from thinking about your destination, the future, regrets related to the past, or projects and concerns not immediately present that may keep your mind spinning, disengaged from your body and this wonderful moment. Once you become familiar with the practice and the texture of your experience, feel free to invent phrases you find particularly helpful or inspiring.

Bringing It Home

You can practice walking with these phrases or coordinating your steps with your breath any time you find yourself walking—from your house to the car, from the car to work, down the hallway to the bathroom, going into the doctor's or dentist's office, or while out walking your dog—to help you return to the present moment. The body is always an invitation to be here, now.

CHAPTER THREE

Bringing All Our Senses to Life

An Addict on the Trail

PHAP XA

Four years after Brother Phap Luu and I decided to lead an extended mindful backpacking retreat on the Appalachian Trail, the idea had become reality. At the beginning of April 2018, a group of monastics and enthusiastic participants began hiking directly from one of our retreat centers, Blue Cliff Monastery in upstate New York. The retreat would last for seven weeks; participants would rotate each week, but the guiding monastic team would remain constant as we hiked from New York to Washington, DC. We hoped to arrive at the National Mall by the end of May to sit where Thay had sat in meditation with more than a hundred World Bank staff members six years prior. In doing so, we wanted to offer the support of our collective mindful presence to a nation that seemed caught in ever-deeper turmoil.

We set some ground rules about phone use. Following these guidelines, I use an app on a cell phone without a SIM card to help the group navigate during our second week on the trail. Though finding the white blazes that mark the trail isn't difficult, we also have to look for suitable places to take breaks, fill up our water bottles, and set up camp for the night. The app makes all of this easier. Since we split into two hiking groups during the day, Lazy Monk—Brother Phap Khoi's nickname—also has a phone. His has reception, and he occasionally uses it to contact the other hiking group or Mama Sue (Phap Luu's actual mom!), who helps with organizational details and drives a support vehicle.

During the orientation at the start of the retreat, Brother Phap Luu and I had explained to the group how we'd use these two cell phones—the group only needed one navigational phone and one connected phone for emergencies, so everyone else could just take a digital break and enjoy their mindful practice in the woods. We encouraged participants not to use their phones so they could focus on being in touch with themselves, with nature, and with the other members of the group. Occasionally someone might use their phone to take a picture, which was fine. The main point was for hikers not to distract themselves with their phones or use them to avoid noticing physical or emotional discomfort. Our pain, anxiety, and despair need our presence and attention to transform.

For Henry, one of the hikers on retreat this week, setting aside his phone is especially difficult. Most weeks of the retreat, we tend to experience a participant or two having trouble letting their phones rest, and this week it's Henry. During every break, he whips out his phone to check the news. About three days into his week-long retreat, Henry gets tired and starts to complain nonstop. "Who thought of this stupid idea of a hiking retreat?" Lazy Monk hears him say.

It's amazing to me, a modern monk who grew up in a largely analog world—I was born in 1974—how quickly people have gotten addicted to digital media and cell phones. A word has even been coined—nomophobia[4]—to describe the fear of being without a mobile phone. Our addiction to being connected to the internet comes at a cost, though. It often means we're not present for the people around us, much less for ourselves or our surroundings.

On the trail, Henry's compulsion to check the news seems to fuel his mood swings. His engagement with his screen as well as his emotional volatility weighs on the group. Noticing this, we monastics commit to consciously staying connected to Henry with kind words and gentle smiles. We hope to create an environment that will help draw Henry out of the bubble of his phone. For Henry, and for all the hikers, connecting to the natural elements and allowing themselves to be nourished through all their senses is the heart of the retreat.

During the two decades I've spent as a monk, I've witnessed many people going through darkness: grief from the loss of a loved one, tension at work, pain over a recent divorce, the numberless other difficulties that at some point or another cast a shadow over our lives. For me, being able to offer support just by being there and listening has been one of the most fulfilling parts of being a monk. I hardly have to say anything, I've realized. Just offering space to speak and be listened to is of immeasurable value. This week on the Appalachian Trail, I feel something going on under the surface for Henry and try to hold that space for him. As the week goes on, he never explicitly asks for help. I sense that he deeply longs for connection, yet doesn't quite know how to seek or ask for it. Perhaps burying his nose in his phone frees him from having to figure a way out or risk hurt feelings.

It surprises us all, then, when Henry suddenly exclaims one evening, "This is just beautiful!" He'd just sat down at the end of a long day of complaining. As he looks around the group, he expresses appreciation for our company, our surroundings, and the present moment. I can scarcely believe my ears. Perhaps something has shifted for Henry. Perhaps the trees have pulled him in despite his addictive phone behavior, or the collective group mindfulness has seeped through. Whatever the process, for a moment at least, Henry's distraction falls away, and he waters the seeds of presence and joy in himself and others.

No Inside No Outside

PHAP LUU

Before becoming a monk, I undertook a one-week Zen retreat in New England. We practiced sitting and walking meditation in the meditation hall for more than nine hours a day. In the evening, after our meal and before the final sitting and chanting session, I would explore the nearby network of forest trails. The intensive experience of alternating sitting and walking meditation day after day calmed and transformed my mind. Walking through the woods, I would feel there was no me: all the stories I'd told myself about who I was, what I'd done, and where I was going revealed themselves to be just that — stories.

One night I took a trail that opened onto a field which bordered a country road, and when the black sky, speckled with stars and the spray of the Milky Way, appeared through the forest canopy, every attachment I had to concepts of space and time dissolved within me. I couldn't even say there was this present moment, that there *was* anything. The experience was complete and whole, with no sense of separation between "inside" and "outside," "future" and "past," "body" and "mind."

Fortunately, by then I'd had enough blissful, meditation-supported experiences to know not to get too attached to this one. I wasn't surprised when my usual litany of afflictions returned: anger, sensual desire, jealousy, and so on. Yet that experience in the woods has been a guiding light for me, a comfort and a beacon on many less peaceful nights.

On Awareness

Most of our evolutionary history hasn't been one of felt isolation but rather, one of immersion and integration: we've been able to see, smell, and hear directly with our senses what's good for us and where potential dangers lie. However, given the modern complexity of our lives, immersed as we are by various means and media in a sea of thousands of people, we are brought to the limit of what we can understand through our senses alone. On a planet with more than eight billion people who have unprecedented freedom of movement and communication—not to mention the now permanent and growing multitude of refugees created by factors including the worsening climate crisis—it's no wonder we sometimes feel lost and even unsure of who we are or which community we belong to.

Yet our human, creaturely senses remain very much a part of our bodies and our lives. Coming back to our breathing and sensing nature within and around us—the air that becomes breath in our bodies, the plants with which we build our cells, the water we drink and release—helps us to better understand the root of our emotions and often-mistaken perceptions in what can otherwise be a busy, overwhelming existence. This contact helps us understand the root of our *being*. It reminds us that, despite how hectic modern life can be, we remain embedded in the natural world of which we're made.

Though feelings of isolation can compound our suffering and sense of being overwhelmed or inadequate, the bedrock truth is that we are not separate. The separation we feel in our daily lives is artificial, a construct of our minds. No matter how shiny, sexy, and powerful our cars may be or how comfortable or magnificent our houses or apartments, we continue to breathe air circulated by trees, to drink water as it moves through its endless natural cycle, and to eat food grown with the help of sun and soil.

Coming back to these realities can be deeply healing. Awareness of our cellular connection to everything around us can be a sword that cuts through the illusion of our felt isolation. When we practice hiking Zen and pay attention to our bodies and our senses from the inside out, we can take refuge in the stability of the earth's capacity to sustain us. When we walk, we can enjoy the contact—the bodily sensation—between our feet and the earth. We can stand still and be aware of what we see, sensing the beauty around us. We can focus on listening—there may be a creek, birds singing, or the sound of our own breathing. As we come back to our senses in the present moment with the support of the ground beneath our feet, the narratives in our heads—stories of our pain from the past, anxiety in the present, or fears for the future—can dissolve.

When there's a storm, we look right away for somewhere to take refuge from the elements. The same is true when the storm is within us, the storm of our fear, anxiety, or depression. We can find refuge, not by running away from our suffering but by learning to turn toward it, to embrace and transform it. When we practice being there for Mother Earth with all our awakened senses, we see we're not separate from the earth; this connection can also be our refuge.

It is not enough to have deep insight; true insight naturally leads to action. Engaged Buddhism means we don't just study Zen teachings as a philosophy; we apply them right away in our daily lives — individually, as communities, and in our work as activists and agents of transformation in the world. We act, with our bodies, our speech, and our thoughts, all of which are interconnected. Skillful action comes out of love, a love we feel for all species — including the human species — and our planet. It does not come from despair. Love is insight, love is understanding. This is the fertile soil in which our actions want to grow.

When we see clear-cut forests, mines like open wounds facing the sky, and kilometers of plastic trash floating in the ocean, we know we haven't yet learned — or we've forgotten — to take refuge in Mother Earth. We're not as small and insignificant as we may think; we're an integral part of one great planet. Our stability and capacity for transformation and healing are beyond comprehension. When we touch this reality, our deep roots in the planet come alive — the roots we share with our spiritual, blood, and land ancestors. We're not just an individual drop of water; we're a whole river.

Healing begins when we see the harm our species has done to the earth and touch the seed of compassion within ourselves instead of falling into despair and anger. Our pride, our ambition, and our desires have led us to the current planetary crisis. With our senses alive and the insight that we and the earth are literally one, we recognize that our healing and transformation are only possible alongside the healing and transformation of all beings and of the planet itself. Our practice takes on urgency when we realize that the converse is also true: the healing of the earth is only possible when we heal ourselves.

Opening Our Senses

Look for a quiet place outside—it could be at the foot of a tree, in an open field, leaning against a rock in the desert, at a park, or anywhere else available to you. You may like to take a moment, in whatever way feels best, to ask permission to sit, acknowledging the presence of your surroundings—Zen monks and nuns often do this with a heartfelt bow. If we like, we can ring a small bell at the beginning of our practice to help us focus on listening and settle into the moment.

We sit comfortably upright. It is easiest to do this if there is a little bit of a slope so we can cross our legs with our knees lower than our hips. If you can't find a slope, you can sit on your shoes or your coat to make it easier to sit upright. This posture helps us maintain attention and feel alive in our practice. If you get tired, you can lean against a tree or anything else nearby, allowing your body to relax and feel energized by the vitality of the forest or landscape around you. Then, engage in this practice:

Be aware of your posture and body, upright but relaxed. Relax your eyes, keeping a soft gaze gently focused on the earth in front of you. You can also close your eyes. Become aware of the smells and sounds around you. Become aware of your in- and out-breath. The breath can serve as an anchor in meditation, helping you to focus on the present moment. You can cultivate this awareness by repeating the following words to yourself, coordinating them with your breath:

> *Breathing in, I know I am breathing in. Breathing out, I know I am breathing out.*
>
> *In / Out.*

Continue matching verbal cues with your breath to help your attention settle and your senses come alive:

> *Breathing in, I am aware of my skin. Breathing out, I am aware of the contact my skin makes with the soil, the air, and my clothing.*
>
> *Aware of skin / Contact with soil, air, clothing.*
>
> *Breathing in, I am aware of my nose and the wonderful fragrances in nature: the smell of earth, the fresh air after rain. Breathing out, I smile to the wondrous scents of the natural world.*
>
> *Aware of smells / Smiling to smells.*
>
> *Breathing in, I am aware of the taste in my mouth. Breathing out, I smile to taste sensations.*
>
> *Aware of taste / Smiling to taste.*
>
> *Breathing in, I am aware of sound: the song of birds, the babbling of a brook, the wind rustling leaves. Breathing out, I smile to the wondrous sounds of life.*
>
> *Aware of sounds / Smiling to sounds.*

Breathing in, I am aware of the millions of colors I see with my eyes. Breathing out, I smile to the brilliant colors of nature.

Aware of color / Smiling to nature's beauty.

Breathing in, I'm aware of my thoughts. Breathing out, I smile to my mind.

Aware of thoughts / Smiling to mind.

You may like to follow all these steps or to practice with two or three senses at a time. Practicing like this in the natural world, we're closer to the stimuli our senses have evolved to receive. Slowly moving through an awareness of each sense helps us understand how stimuli affect our mood and are a kind of "food." Until we develop the habit of recognizing how we feed ourselves through our senses, we can't understand how our emotions arise. The solidity we develop in such outdoor practices can leave us better prepared to cope with and understand our sensory stimuli in more artificial, constructed environments. We can be aware that many generations have found support in practicing this way—outside, interwoven with nature. We're part of nature, and we're connected to the earth, to the trees, the air, and all other beings. Please don't take our word for it—see for yourself if this is true.

Bringing It Home

Our senses are with us everywhere we go, and every moment is a good moment to turn our attention toward them. You may choose certain sounds or situations in your daily life to remind you to stop what you're doing and bring your full attention to one of your senses for five or ten seconds. In our Zen centers, for example, we have clocks that chime every fifteen minutes. When we hear the chime, everyone stops and comes back to what's going on in their senses in the present moment. If you don't have such a clock, you can download the Plum Village app on your phone and set the bell to sound every fifteen minutes or half hour.

Other cues in our daily lives can help us come back to our sense of the present moment. While driving, a red light can remind us to come back to ourselves and our breathing. Instead of just waiting for the green light, we can immediately smile and relax our facial muscles, breathe deeply, lean back in our seat, relax our shoulders, and feel the rising and falling of our abdomen. This is a deep relearning, a true training; normally, we're stressed out when we come to a red light. Our impulse is to get frustrated and annoyed that we can't continue toward where we want to go. Recognizing this impulse to rush, deciding to let go of it, and training ourselves to see the red light as a friend inviting us to come back to embodied awareness of the present moment can be deceptively powerful. We invite you to experiment with this practice in your daily life and notice what occurs.

CHAPTER FOUR

Being Comfortable with the Uncomfortable

Conscious of the Cold

PHAP LUU

On the second evening of our Appalachian Trail retreat, I set up my hammock in an idyllic spot just uphill from a bend in a stream, suspended over loose rocks across from a crowd of hemlock firs. Usually within minutes of entering the hammock, the down in the quilt radiates back the heat from my body and that, combined with similar heat-reflection from the top quilt, makes for a warm cocoon in which to pass the night, swaying in cozy peace. This time, just fifteen minutes after zipping myself into the hammock, I'm aware of a spot of cold expanding on my back around my kidneys. Up and out again in the dark, I fiddle with the elastic cords and their tiny carabiners, unravel them, and tie them shorter on the main line to cinch the underquilt tighter to the underside of the hammock.

Back in the hammock twenty minutes later, I detect another pocket of cold air under the other side of my back. Hopping out again, I adjust the cords and pull on the rope running through spring-loaded fasteners at the ends of the underquilt to now cinch the ends of the quilt. The situation improves, but it's still not the warmth I'd experienced during previous nights.

A piercing wind descends along the streambed with renewed force, and no matter how I adjust my bedding, the wind still manages to thrust its way through the interstices of the underquilt and the hammock. I wake again, breathe in and out, and shiver with the thought, "My body is cold." Sleeping through this cold is clearly impossible, and I need to empty my bladder anyhow, so I unzip the bug fly, slip on my boots, put on my jacket, and walk a few minutes down the forest trail with a flashlight. The thick, dark air saps the precious warmth from my body. There is no sign of the moon. After relieving myself, I try to bring mindfulness to my whole body.

I know I can't go back to sleep in this state. I need to do something to create enough body heat for the down quilt to reflect. The ground is too uneven to run safely, even with a light, and so I think: jumping jacks! I find a stable piece of ground in the middle of the track and begin jumping up and down, spreading and closing my arms and legs in rhythm to the jump, more than fifty times—enough to get my blood moving, but not so much that I start sweating.

I've learned most of what I know about how to live simply in the forest from camping trips as a Boy Scout: how to tie a bowline (with one hand!), split wood with an ax, cook fish on stone in a fire, build a makeshift shelter, and kindle a flame without matches. When I was about twelve, the scoutmaster planned a trip specifically to teach us winter camping. When the Saturday arrived, we met as usual at the parking lot of the Methodist Church. The temperature had dropped drastically and the predicted wind chill that weekend was thirty degrees below freezing. At one point on our hike, after walking through the snow for over an hour, my hands were so numb I couldn't even unzip my backpack to get at a granola bar. Red-haired, freckle-faced Jason Pease, one of my friends, had to do it for me. I'd never felt so cold, for so long, in my life. As night fell, the troop set up camp, but my slender, shivering body couldn't imagine passing the dark hours exposed to such cold with only the thin walls of a tent and measly sleeping bag to protect me. Fred, one of the volunteer adult leaders, also couldn't handle the cold, so I sat with him and one other boy in a car by the campsite, the idling engine pumping heat into the metallic bubble of the cab. *What would happen? Would we stay there all night, sleeping in the car?*

Standing in the dark on the Appalachian Trail decades later, my heart still pumping warmth from the jumping jacks, hot shame returns to my face as I remember asking to call my father to come pick me up. Later, the scoutmaster told my father that the troop, which also broke camp and went home after my capitulating call, could have spent the night, if only I hadn't called home. Ever since, I've been determined to learn to bear the cold despite my thin body. When I learned meditation, my determination doubled: I threw myself into ice cold, spring thaw streams and did hour-long sitting meditation sessions in freezing conditions outside to see what cold I could tolerate while remaining focused on my breathing.

Some long, slow hours after my jumping jacks, I wake to the rising sun's rays radiating through the bare limbs of trees to warm my face. I peer through my bug net to see Brother Dao Hanh beside the other hikers, calmly eating his breakfast. His cheeks redden when he catches my eyes—I've slept through sitting meditation! At the close of dinner the night before, I had been the one who set the 6 a.m. time for all of us to sit together. I assume Brother Dao Hanh is embarrassed that I, the senior monk and supposed leader of the group, slept in—right in front of everyone.

Sheepish yet mustering some sense of decorum, I unzip the hammock and stand in the full glow of the morning sun. Breathing in and out, I practice embracing my unpleasant feelings of self-judgment. My body starts to relax. I feel a little compassion toward myself: planning and preparing for this trip had made me more tired than I'd anticipated. Still, as I make my way toward the group—who are now chowing down on oatmeal—I find myself mumbling apologies. Their eyes twinkle with amusement. Soon I realize they're just fine, eating breakfast. Everyone had wanted to let me sleep in—empathizing, perhaps, with all I'd done to get the trip off the ground over the past few days.

I smile at the humor of the situation: the monk set to lead sitting meditation had been left to sleep in, thanks to the compassion of others. The consensus of the group, anyhow, is that it had been far too cold to sit that morning. Even now, basking in a bit of sun, I notice some of them struggling to grip their spoons in the frigid air. I join them with my bowl, happy to notice I've become better at being comfortable with the uncomfortable.

Simple Living in Nature
PHAP XA

Backpacking or spending time outside can be uncomfortable: we may be out in the rain the entire day, the pack can feel like a burden, the nights might be bitterly cold, and sometimes finding a suitable spot to sleep is a struggle. On our mindful hiking retreats over the years, we've experienced all of this.

Given a choice, I'd opt for sunny days, cool nights, and flat, mossy campsites beside fresh streams every night. Since this isn't possible, I try to accept everything as it comes, humbly aware there are many things I cannot change. Looking back,

I appreciate all the discomfort I have experienced. After a week in the forest eating mostly dehydrated food, a simple meal with fresh vegetables tastes like heaven, and being in a warm, dry place where we can wash our clothes and relax becomes a deep pleasure rather than something taken for granted.

In my early twenties, I biked five hundred miles from my home in the Netherlands to Switzerland with John, a friend from university. We passed through the Black Forest in Southern Germany, riding up and down rolling, forested hills the entire day. It was so beautiful! I enjoyed being in nature, breathing fresh mountain air, just being outside and biking. The surroundings deeply imprinted themselves in my mind.

At night during that trip, lying in the tent with my eyes closed, my mind would fill with images of green trees and the sounds of the forest. I'd been in contact with the trees all day. As I waited for sleep, nothing but nature occupied me: no thoughts about the past or the future, no projects, no plans. Just trees. Birdsong. Wind. Clouds. It felt perfect. I experienced a deep sense of belonging, at home and in harmony with the natural world that had sheltered and sustained thousands of generations before me.

One day, as we rode along the Rhine, it just kept raining and raining. We were completely soaked. John wanted to pay for a hotel to avoid setting up camp in the rain. When we came to a town, we split up to search for a room. I felt so embarrassed about approaching the reception desk of a fancy, clean hotel in my smelly, sopping bike outfit that I decided not to look at all. Instead, I just waited for John to come back. He returned without having found anything either, so we decided to go on in the streaming rain until we arrived at a campsite an hour later.

The campsite owner must have felt sorry for us—she pointed to a little wooden shed open on one side, just big enough for our two sleeping mats. Happy, grateful, and exhausted, we rolled out our mats, removed our wet clothes, crawled into our warm, dry sleeping bags, and fell asleep. That night, the simple shed, the fresh, clean air, and the relaxing sound of rain falling on the roof was better than any five-star hotel.

This simplicity, so deeply nourishing in our modern world, is something we deliberately cultivate on our retreats. It is, of course, not something we invented—Zen has its roots in the simple, happy life of the Buddha. Having recognized that wealth alone doesn't lead to true peace and freedom, the Buddha (who had been born a prince but left all luxuries behind) voluntarily lived most of his adult life with the bare minimum of possessions. He didn't long for anything more; at ease with himself and his environment, taking refuge in the forest as his dwelling place, he and his community practiced being present and alive in every moment, and this made him feel free.

Comfort is different from happiness. I didn't become a monk out of a need for comfort. Ironically, being too comfortable can make it more difficult to feel at peace. When I arrived in Plum Village in southwestern France to ordain in 2002, the monastery's muddy walking paths and old drafty limestone farmhouses were far from comfortable. But in my heart, I felt a deep sense of belonging, of being home. Plum Village holds the same sense of joy in a simple life as a warm, dry shed on a rainy day.

On Comfort (or Lack Thereof)

It's okay to feel uncomfortable sometimes, physically or emotionally. The pain indicates something we need to attend to. Pain isn't always dangerous. When we're in pain or discomfort, our tendency is to react with a fight, freeze, or flight response to make the discomfort disappear. Such a reaction just adds stress. We can choose instead to return to our breathing, calm our body and mind, and embrace the discomfort with mindfulness. If you're outside (or inside) and notice you're feeling uncomfortable, can you take a few moments to simply stop and be with the feeling? What sensations do you notice in your body? Can you feel the ground beneath your feet? Is the wind blowing across your skin? What's your breath doing? Our bodies know how to be alive to the present moment. By embracing discomfort with mindfulness, we unlearn patterns of anxiety and depression and become reacquainted with our natural capacity to heal.

Many of us no longer feel comfortable in the forest or under the open sky. Feelings of discomfort or agitation can be an invitation to look more closely at our way of living. It is inevitable that all of us at some point experience moments or long stretches of being uncomfortable in our bodies. Noticing such uncomfortable sensations as they arise outdoors, we can train ourselves to relax within discomfort.

We can look at our body and our feelings throughout the day in both artificial and natural environments and observe the effect of the physical world on our personal happiness and well-being. When we step into nature, can we be truly present for our surroundings? Can we train our mind to let go of its chatter? When our ancestors in the forest were unmindful, it lowered their chances of survival. Being present was a matter of life or death. Though most of us don't need to look for food when we're out in nature, being present *can* still be the difference between health and injury—even between life and death. You may notice, for example, that if you're not present when you make your way through forest undergrowth, if you're caught in your thinking, you may trip on a stone, a root, or a patch of mud and injure yourself. A painful experience can mirror for us our mind's distraction.

Moving with awareness outside, this dance of *training through untraining*, involves both body and mind. Whether on a self-guided hour-long walk or an extended hiking retreat, physical discomfort may arise. Physically, you can prepare a stable foundation by keeping yourself healthy, yet it's inevitable that you will experience moments of pain or discomfort. Mentally, the practice of mindfulness trains you to relax in your body and trust it.

In our aspiration to become comfortable with the uncomfortable, we can consider how external circumstances may support us. Time of day, for example, can impact our capacity to train mentally and physically—earlier in the day, people tend to have their best energy. This may be a time when it's easier to enjoy walking in silence, for example. You may have a greater ability to notice your experience and remain present with its inevitable ups and downs. When we're tired, we tend to turn toward talking to distract ourselves from our exhaustion, both physical and emotional.

Stopping talking, however, can help to quiet the mind and support your ability to recognize what's happening over time. Without external conversation occupying you, you can give all your attention to what's going on in the present moment, both in and around you. This is why training both the body and the mind is an essential part of hiking Zen. With more practice and as your body adjusts and becomes more capable, you may be able to maintain a relaxed and steady pace in peaceful silence for longer, regardless of the time of day. This will support your ability to become comfortable with the uncomfortable, to free yourself from the habit of turning away from every little agitation that arises.

When we feel emotional discomfort, we can practice mindfulness of the body to reestablish peace. More than two decades into the twenty-first century, we find the world mired in environmental, economic, and political crises that can make every act of daily life emotionally and ethically uncomfortable — what we eat, how and where we travel, where we work, and how our implicit biases affect our interactions. When our mindful breathing and walking is well established, we are prepared to embrace uncertainty in our daily lives and learn how to respond in a heartfelt way to discomfiting emotions. With our planet soon to host nine billion people, learning to take care of uncomfortable feelings and bring harmony to our daily interactions is essential.

PRACTICE

Embracing Pain and Discomfort

Though there's often nothing as obvious as rain, cold, or strenuous exertion to challenge us, turning toward our internal landscape is foundational to hiking Zen — walking in freedom. In fact, sometimes physical discomfort can build our capacity to be with deeper kinds of turmoil or overwhelming feelings. After we've experienced riding the waves of the physical challenges that confront us on the trail and come out whole, perhaps even stronger, on the other side, we may have more confidence in our ability to do the same with our emotions or internal discomfort.

Here's a practice you can do whenever you find yourself in pain or discomfort. Whatever the position of your

body—walking, standing, sitting, or lying down—come
back to your breathing and practice the following:

> *Breathing in, I know I'm breathing in. Breathing out,
> I know I'm breathing out.*
>
> *In / Out.*
>
> *Breathing in, I recognize the physical pain and discom-
> fort in me. Breathing out, I smile to the pain and discom-
> fort in me.*
>
> *Recognizing pain / Smiling to pain.*
>
> *Breathing in, I recognize the emotions that arise when
> I'm in pain and discomfort. Breathing out, I smile to the
> emotions.*
>
> *Recognizing emotion / Smiling to emotion.*
>
> *Breathing in, I stop feeding my emotions by thinking
> and complaining. Breathing out, I'm in touch with the
> raw sensation of pain or discomfort without adding
> thoughts or complaints.*
>
> *Stopping the feeding of emotions / Aware of the
> pain.*
>
> *Breathing in, I am aware of tension in my body and
> mind. Breathing out, I let go of the tension in my body
> and mind.*
>
> *Aware of tension / Letting go.*

Breathing in, I see I have more than enough conditions for happiness. I focus on the parts of my body not experiencing pain or discomfort. Breathing out, I smile to the conditions of happiness within me and around me.

Conditions for happiness / Smiling.

When you learn this practice well, it can work in any uncomfortable situation. Embracing difficult, uncomfortable emotions or sensations and learning to stop feeding them can help you avoid saying or doing things that make the situation worse.

Bringing It Home

The practice of shining the light of mindfulness on discomfort can be applied every time we experience pain—whether physical or mental—in our daily lives. When we eat too much, we may get a stomachache. Bringing awareness to this helps us to stop putting more food in our mouth. When we wake up and don't feel rested, we can embrace our drowsiness with mindfulness. With time, we may adjust our evenings—removing electronic devices and televisions from our sleeping space or practicing sitting meditation for fifteen minutes before we lie down, for example—to respond to our discomfort so we feel ready to sleep. When we sit too long at a desk, awareness of discomfort can motivate us to stand up, stretch, go for a walk, or even just to gaze out the window for a few moments. Many moments in our daily lives offer opportunities to become comfortable with the uncomfortable so we can respond skillfully to the present moment.

When you experience discomfort—anger or sadness, for example—as the result of a conversation, try embracing that discomfort with mindfulness by taking time to breathe and be present with the emotion. Maybe you can stop yourself from reacting or lashing out in response. Feeling rushed is another kind of discomfort. When you hurry from one place to another, notice what this produces in your body. How does your experience of a meeting change depending on whether you rush to get there versus if you walk in with calm, unhurried steps? With mindfulness, discomfort becomes a stimulus for change in our behavior.

CHAPTER FIVE:

Transforming Strong Emotions

Heavy Rain in Maryland

PHAP LUU

The rain increases as we step over the dangling wire strung between posts to close the gravel track to traffic. Day thirty-nine on the Appalachian Trail. Day two of steady rain in Frederick County, Maryland, where there is a flood watch. The patter of raindrops on the leaves overhead has increased to a monotonous drone. I smile to keep my mind cheerful at the prospect of pitching camp in a downpour.

In drier times, our campground would have been a haven. Today I feel trapped as we huddle under the overhang of the toilet block and peer out at the square cinder plots enclosed by wooden planks that designate each campsite. Our reluctance is palpable.

The public bathroom—toilets, showers, heat, and mirrors— quickly becomes our dry oasis and common room. Ramon and I strike out in the rain to claim one cinder square with a dilapidated picnic table as our own and then proceed to scout nearby trees to hang our hammocks. By now, with six weeks of backpacking behind me, I've learned to secure the tarp first to keep the hammock dry while I hang it.

57

"Let's raise a tarp over the table," I suggest once our hammocks are in place, envisioning a dry space to move around in.

"There's too much rain," says Ramon. "Let's just eat under our hammocks."

I won't let go of my idea, though. As I start to list reasons why we should hang a tarp, Ramon shrugs and joins me in search of an adequate dead branch to serve as our center post.

But now we're getting even wetter, though I hadn't thought it possible, and I feel wild with exhilaration from the storm. Once we find a dead tree limb, I begin tying trucker's hitches with slip knots in the tarp's strings as a makeshift block and tackle—two on each of the four corners of the tarp to balance the poles and render the structure taut and stable. Twenty minutes later we sit at the table, out of reach of the rain, though we're already soaked to the skin. Ramon excuses himself to take a shower.

Darting between the tarp and my hammock twenty yards away, I take stock of my remaining dry clothes. One set of short upper robes and pants remain dry—spared the rain that seeped into the inner recesses of my pack. Guarding them carefully, I set out under an umbrella to my own shower.

Tarps, socks, and sundry clothes are strung like Christmas decorations across the room. Boots line the walls. The showers flow at full tilt, with only one unoccupied. Steam rises like clouds and as I lather my body under a hot torrent of water, I feel warmth spreading through my aching, chilled limbs and revel in how an everyday experience like a hot shower can become a treasured blessing after days walking in wet, raw woods. In the cold I was happy: I had been enjoying these wet days, yet I feel even happier now, pulling on dry clothes and carefully protecting my new comfort as I head out into the rain.

Back at the makeshift sanctuary, Ramon, warm and chipper after his own shower, pipes up with his usual "Bouillon?" as he smiles over his boiling pot. Dry and content in the middle of the full downpour around us, I reach forward to accept the steaming broth. As Ramon hands me the silicone mug, the bottom catches on the weather-warped edge of one of the table planks. I've just raised my hands to receive the mug when, in a split second, it tips in his hands and hot broth spills over me, a heated waterfall gushing onto and through the last, thin monastic slacks I'd so zealously kept dry. Immediately, my dreams of a cozy night are extinguished. The savory, umami vegetable bouillon that has revitalized me countless times in the past six weeks when I was cold, when I was thirsty, when I very much needed something hot, now undeniably spreads not through my body, warming my belly as it should—a gesture of kindness and brotherhood on Ramon's part—but heedlessly over my lap.

From the depths of my being comes the urge to scream: a primal, irrepressible impulse. If there's a candidate for trail angel, for a complete bodhisattva who selflessly looks out for the well-being of the entire group, who steps up at any moment to help someone with a blister, someone needing water, someone setting up a hammock, it's Ramon. Nevertheless, my anger, primal, yet mine and my responsibility, rises inexorably.

"These are the only dry pants I have left!" I growl, unable to conceal my intense displeasure and wanting to lay the blame somewhere.

Fortunately, years of practice help me restrain myself and result in a single insight: just as infinite parallel strands of possible futures collapse into one in every moment, what I think, say, and do with this anger will collapse the possible into the realized. Depending on how I act, my anger could cause harm to others and, in the long run, even greater harm to myself.

As I stand beside the table, breathing in and out, my emotional response begins to pass. Ramon's repentant look both acknowledges my shock and seeks pardon. I know soon we'll be laughing. The situation *is* absurd—rain, wet clothes and equipment, and now vegetable broth in my lap, already cool and damp on my legs. I breathe while recognizing anger's presence, embrace it in my body, and let go. Anger won't change the situation for the better; it could, however, make it worse. I resolve not to let the anger say or do something I'd later regret and instead focus on all the conditions for happiness still present. My upper robe, for example, isn't wet from the spill, nor is the T-shirt beneath it.

Ramon looks truly contrite, so I say some reassuring words, letting him know I'll be all right. Beneath my umbrella, I make my way to my hammock and, under the fly, take off my upper robe and pants, then tie the upper robe around my waist like a skirt. I look silly, but I'm dry and decent enough to go out in public. By the time I return to the picnic table, Ramon is smiling again, I'm smiling, and we do laugh. Our brotherhood—so deep throughout the whole trip—didn't crack or waver in the heat of my anger. Though anger is an intense, compelling emotion, I experience once again the truth that it's possible to transform emotion instead of transmitting it. When we learn to do this in our personal interactions, we build a foundation for doing this in the larger world.

Emotional Alchemy

PHAP XA

Walking meditation can transform strong emotions, even emotions as powerful as anger or rage. I don't believe this because my teacher told me so. I believe it because it has been my experience.

I remember the first time I fully experienced this alchemy. In 2003, a few months after my ordination as a young novice monk,

I got incredibly angry at one of my monastic brothers. It was on a Day of Mindfulness, a day when the whole monastic and surrounding lay (non-monastic) community gathers to practice together through seated meditation, discussion, walking meditation, and group sharing. Everyone had gathered in the Lower Hamlet of Plum Village, where the monastic sisters live. The day had been rich and nourishing, and I was just about to walk the few miles back to Upper Hamlet, where the brothers live. Some of us brothers and sisters were casually standing together exchanging goodbyes. In that moment of relaxed friendliness, suddenly one of my monastic brothers made fun of me. His barb left me humiliated and upset, completely in the grip of very different emotions than I'd been feeling a few seconds earlier.

Right away, I felt a very strong impulse to react with anger, to give my anger a voice. I felt a wave of heat wash over me, and I wanted to say or do something to hurt my brother in revenge. Luckily, though, thanks to the practices I was learning as a monk in training, I noticed this impulse and decided to take care of the anger instead of acting on it.

Easier said than done. My heart pounded; I felt enraged. I slowly turned and started walking back to Upper Hamlet by myself, paying careful attention to my steps and my breathing. I usually didn't walk so slowly, but I knew I had to take good care of myself and restore peace in my body and mind. As I walked, a negative and violent movie played ceaselessly in my head, stuck in a never-ending loop that showed my perceived humiliation over and over. Mentally, I couldn't resist going over the situation again and again: What options had I had? How could I have reacted to make myself feel less vulnerable and helpless?

Step, breath, step, breath. Again and again, I returned to the practice of mindful walking. And then, after about fifteen minutes, a thought rang out: "I am not helpless!" Just like that,

I could fully enjoy the rest of the walk. I was no longer a victim of my own anger. I felt light and free, no longer compulsively thinking about the event or held hostage by my anger. Intense happiness and freshness now accompanied each step.

This experience gave me a living faith that the practice of mindful breathing and walking can help us process our strong emotions. People frequently say, "You need to move on" from painful events. Walking meditation gives us a way not to turn away from pain, but to literally, physically and mentally, move onward from painful points in our lives.

Walking back to Upper Hamlet that day, now feeling free and light, I cautiously turned my mind again to my recent experience of humiliation. If I touched the wound, would it open again? This time, though, I didn't get angry, and I didn't feel humiliated. My anger had truly receded. In its place, I saw my brother more clearly; I could think of several reasons why he might have said the words I found so hurtful. Inwardly, I smiled at him and his words, no longer believing he'd intended to hurt me. Walking meditation helped me to recognize my hurt feeling and after being with it, to transform it. Now I could preserve my relationship with my monastic brother while behaving in a way respectful to myself. At that moment, I felt so much compassion for myself as a sensitive, feeling being.

I feel grateful, in retrospect, that I didn't punch him or respond tit for tat with a cutting remark. That wouldn't have been taking care of my anger at all, and I would have missed the opportunity to learn and deepen my practice. Now, more than twenty years later, the memory of the exact circumstances has faded, but the feeling of painful emotions becoming happiness is as vivid as if it happened yesterday. The engaged practice of compassion, of seeing the hurt child both in myself and in others, is a powerful response whose impact deepens with time.

Often in our daily lives we feel like we don't have the time to care for strong, unpleasant emotions. Perhaps we haven't experienced the powerful joy and freedom that can come from the practices of mindful breathing and walking and the transformation they make possible. On our mindful hiking retreats, all of us have a special opportunity to make space to be with our emotions, whatever arises. Away from the daily hustle and bustle, immersed in the natural cycles around us, it's possible to train our minds to take a different path when strong emotions inevitably arise. Together with fellow hikers, we can sense how the natural world—the earth holding us up, the wind breathing fresh life into our bodies, the sun offering warmth for growth and vitality—can support this deep practice. Ultimately, our life can be a string of transformative moments that make us who we are and create what we are able to offer.

On Recognizing Emotions

Our feelings flow like a river: always present, always changing. Feelings can be pleasant, unpleasant, or neutral, and we can train ourselves to recognize them with equanimity, without judgment. This mindful awareness is the first step toward true freedom. Recognizing our emotions and their qualities allows us to *choose* how we respond, aware of what impact our response might have.

How might we respond to pleasant feelings, for example? When we bring awareness to a pleasant feeling, like the joy we feel when we meet a long-lost friend, the pleasant feeling can increase. Our mindfulness strengthens the seed of joy. We're aware that life is always changing, that it's not certain we will see this friend again, and this awareness increases our joy, benefiting not only our own well-being but flowing out to others.

When we have an unpleasant feeling, we can decide to be fully present for the feeling without trying to cover it up or push it away. If we observe carefully how we respond to an unpleasant feeling, we may notice such habits as consuming the news, the internet, social media, food, alcohol, sugar, or starting an argument to drive it away. With mindfulness, we can take a moment to stop. Then, often, a different response becomes possible.

In the Plum Village Engaged Buddhist tradition, we sometimes add a fourth kind of feeling: mixed feelings that contain elements both pleasant and unpleasant. If somebody massages us and discovers a knot in our muscles, for example, the massage may hurt. And yet we say, "Please continue. It's painful, but please continue." At times, hiking in nature can bring up mixed feelings—the joy of being out of doors and moving our body might ebb and flow with the pain of trudging along with a heavy backpack.

If a feeling is overwhelming, it may be all we can do just to remove ourselves from the difficult situation and take refuge in nature. Even when it seems like the difficult feeling will never end, it is possible to find moments to be aware of our breath and our steps. Try this for yourself, and see what happens.

Walking meditation, inside or outside, is a wonderful practice to take care of strong emotions. We learn to take refuge in our mindful steps and not in our stories. The stories in our heads may be narratives of victimhood; they may circle around the wish to retaliate or act immediately. In walking meditation or mindful hiking, we train our mind with our body to fortify a habit of not reacting impulsively to strong emotions. Instead, we develop an ability to take care of these emotions so we can respond skillfully to our circumstances rather than just unmindfully reacting.

Often our view of reality is overly simplistic. If we practice well to take care of our anger and bring peace to our body and mind, we may find the stability to look deeply into the nuances of our tendency to become angry and blame others. In pausing we can notice, for example, that many causes and conditions contribute to our anger—anger is not just one person's "fault." With attention, childhood wounds or the pain passed down to us by our ancestors may become apparent; when such truths surface, the opportunity to care for ourselves in this moment can be deeply transformative.

When we're mindful of anger, we see our anger hurts not only the person we believe to be responsible, but also ourselves. Anger is like a flame that burns everything it touches. The person receiving our anger will go on with their lives, but we must live with the burning ember in our hearts, not knowing when it will flare up again. When we have this insight, we see the urgency of taking care of anger right when it arises.

Walking meditation gives us the opportunity to be in touch with our body. We may notice how the quality of our breathing changes; just by bringing awareness to our breathing, we can calm our breathing. When our breathing becomes calm and harmonious, so does our mind. As we walk, we may feel the solidity of the earth under our feet and realize we can take refuge in this solidity. The earth is there for us; we can entrust ourselves to the earth. We are always held. With each step, we can let go of the idea of separation between us and the earth. In each step we can let go of the idea that we must hold onto our feelings. Each step is a step of liberation and ever more lightness, an expression of love and appreciation. We kiss the earth with our feet. We reconnect with Mother Earth for our healing and transformation.

Noticing Emotions as You Walk

When you notice a strong emotion like anger or sadness, pause and bring mindfulness to it. Our tendency is to continue to think about, even obsess about, the object of our anger or sadness. This feeds the emotion and helps it to grow. Every time we feed our anger, our sadness, or another strong emotion, its roots go deeper into our consciousness. Over time, the emotion can appear more and more easily.

With mindfulness (awareness of what is going on inside of us and around us), we unlearn our habitual ways of responding and learn to embrace the emotion with compassion. We practice not taking refuge in the stories in our heads. Instead, we focus on our breathing and on the stable ground beneath our feet. The following exercise is one way to explore and support this process:

Go outside if you can; you may also do this practice inside if that's the only place available.

Take a moment to notice the earth beneath your feet. How does it feel?

Let your thinking flow through your feet into the earth; release your thoughts, your worries, into the earth. In this way you become grounded and solid.

Come back to your breathing. As you begin to walk, don't hesitate to count your steps, coordinating your in-breath and out-breath with the number of steps you take, if that helps gather your attention. By focusing on the counting, you're not paying attention to the story or perception feeding your anger or sadness.

Continue to keep your attention on your breath or on your feet on the earth as you walk, without falling back into the usual story or perception.

You may like to put your hands on your belly as you walk. Notice how your own touch can bring attention down from your head and support a somatic experience of the emotion in your core.

As you continue with this practice over several minutes, you may notice peaceful spaces between the moments when you are lost in thought, feeding anger or sadness. These are moments when you're at peace with your breathing and your steps. You're not thinking about anything. Practice noticing these spaces — even if they last for just a second — and see if they grow. Can you experience one second of peace, then two, then three, before falling back into thinking and feeling anger or sadness?

After fifteen minutes of practice, you may be able to extend these moments of peace by ten or fifteen seconds. Even in this brief time, you can experience your practice bringing you more calm as you become more able to recognize and respond mindfully to strong emotions.

Bringing It Home

When a strong emotion comes up in our daily lives, we can train ourselves to come back to our breathing and embrace it with mindfulness. If you are an activist or someone working for change, you may be discouraged or become dispirited by the slow pace of change in our systems. Learning how to take care of our frustration and despair is the essential foundation of sustainable activist work or engagement. Thay had to practice mindfulness in every moment during his lifelong path of peace activism. Without mindful breathing and walking, he could not have developed the stability and patience necessary to transform violence in the collective consciousness over a period of decades in the way he did.

Some distance and space—say going for a walk in nature or, if you can't find any other place to be alone, making good use of a place without distractions, even a bathroom stall—can give you the energy and concentration to shine the light of mindfulness on a difficult or painful emotion. Breathe, let the emotion pass, and see if a deeper insight into how to respond to the situation arises. We don't suppress the anger; we stop, recognize, accept, and embrace it. We look deeply into its roots. We honor the anger and stop spoon-feeding it so we can eventually respond with clarity, calm, and intelligence. To do this takes courage.

Every evening before sleep, you may like to review the difficult emotions that came up during the day. You may not have been able to take care of the emotion in the moment, but now you have the space to restore peace in your body and mind by bringing awareness to your breathing. It helps to keep distracting and addictive items like screens—smartphones, computers, televisions—out of your sleeping space to facilitate reflection. We invite you to see what happens if you commit to this practice for a few weeks.

CHAPTER SIX

Thundering Silence

Silent Steps, Open Mind

PHAP LUU

In the sixth week of the Appalachian Trail retreat, we find ourselves climbing the tree-covered ridge at the southernmost tip of South Mountain in Maryland. Here the powerful flow of the Potomac River from the north joins the Shenandoah from the south, and together the waters eventually gouge their way through the ancient uplift of the Blue Ridge Mountains. Though these mountains are now crumbling, about 320 million years ago they included peaks as high as the European Alps are today.

Remnants of this massive uplift are evident as we hike. Looking down at the confluence of the two rivers and their subsequent passage through the Potomac Water Gap, I notice just how much rain has come down in the last few days. The Potomac looks like a wild, frothing beast. Even from our vantage point on the ridge, I can see the river spilling into the trees lining its banks—it looks as if the forest itself is sliding into the flood.

From here it's downhill to the hostel across the river from Harpers Ferry. As we descend the ridge on a switchback trail through forests now lush with the new green growth of May,

Ben, a retreat participant, is on my heels, followed by the rest of the group. We discuss growing organic food on the farm he and his wife live on in Virginia.

"When we moved there, we planted soybeans. But with time we learned the forest didn't want to grow soybeans; it wanted to grow deer."

The First Mindfulness Training[5] of the Plum Village Zen tradition speaks about reverence for life. It reminds us of the suffering brought about by the destruction of life. The intense trauma experienced by animals on factory farms, as well as the impact on the climate of the widespread, toxic emissions associated with the dairy and meat industries, led Thay to ask our community in 2007 to adopt a totally plant-based diet. Previously, we'd committed to being vegetarian but still served dairy products and eggs at our retreats. Thay's compassionate insight and plea had a powerful impact—now, we try our best to serve only plant-based food in our retreats.

The Five Mindfulness Trainings are a contemporary version of the Buddha's Five Precepts, which Thay and the Plum Village community have developed and continue to update. You can think of them as a practical guide for cultivating mindfulness in every part of our lives. Rather than fixed rules, they encourage us to be more aware of our actions, speech, and thoughts.

They focus on five core areas of mindful living. The first training, Reverence for Life, is a commitment to protecting life and transforming violence through compassion and nondiscrimination. The second, True Happiness, helps us be more generous and responsible in our use of resources by recognizing that true happiness arises from understanding. The third, True Love, encourages us to be responsible and respectful in our sexual behavior to support the integrity of relationships and families while embracing diversity in gender and orientation. The fourth training, Loving

HIKING ZEN

Speech and Deep Listening, guides us to foster reconciliation by listening deeply to others and speaking with words that inspire hope and healing. With the fifth, Nourishment and Healing, we train ourselves to consume with mindfulness and avoid toxins. In this way we nourish collective harmony and well-being in our body and mind.

So, when Ben, a longtime practitioner in our tradition, recounts killing two or three deer a year to feed his family, it surprises me. An intense discussion ensues: What does it mean to live off the land? Does it matter that most vegans and vegetarians get their food from industrial production? Is killing a deer who has lived its life in the wild and respectfully using every part of it a better alternative?

As a monk, I'm committed to not kill, but it's always easier to point to the horrors of factory farming than to respond to the few omnivores who do rely on more traditional means of hunting and gathering to sustain themselves.[6] Of course, most people who consume animal products, whether dairy, eggs, milk, or meat, buy these from industrial producers rather than keeping or killing the animal themselves—if everyone exclusively ate meat their family or friends hunted, as Ben does, our world would be a quite different place. Nonetheless, occasionally I do encounter someone like Ben and then inevitably, I'm pulled into an all-consuming conversation.

During our deep sharing as we descend that ridge in Maryland, we completely lose awareness of our steps and our breathing. The pace of the whole group behind us slows down as we do, becoming ever more focused on our conversation. Eventually Steve, another member of the hiking retreat, speaks out, exasperated, and the entire group grinds to a halt.

"We decided this morning to go the sixteen miles to the hostel, but now we've lost our pace. There's a conversation up there I'm also interested in, but I can't participate. Meanwhile, we're slowing down. I feel like we're losing our mindfulness."

Stunned and with a twinge of shame, I turn to Steve. Setting the pace for the group is my responsibility. For the first time on this trip, it feels like someone is questioning the authority of a monk—questioning my authority. Though I squirm uncomfortably inside, I know to keep silent and come back to my breathing. The many times throughout my monastic life when I've found myself caught behind two or three brothers walking and talking together flash through my mind. How frustrating it is to be stuck behind people so immersed in conversation they lose all sense of where they are, what they're doing, and who they're with!

Conversation has its place; it can connect, uplift, heal, and relieve. But in the nonstop chatter of a loud world, if we're always talking, we miss opportunities to direct our attention to the present moment. Conversation isn't only external; our mind takes over when our mouths stop moving. How many hours of the day do we spend in silent conversation with ourselves? The mental activity involved both in speaking and thinking detracts from our capacity to deepen and maintain our mindfulness. Insight arises when we learn to stop feeding mental activity and become aware of what's going on inside of and around us. This is why Thay extended the practice of mindful walking to teach both not-talking while walking and not-thinking while walking.

Thoughts, our internal conversations, depend on our attention. When we turn our awareness fully and continuously to the body and the breath, even while walking, we no longer get lost in current problems and projects, regrets about the past, or worries about the future, whether vocalized or internal. In a way, it's extraordinarily simple. When we take our attention away from our mental activity, we stop thinking. We don't suppress our thinking. We remove its essential nutriment—attention—to end confusion in our mind and allow insight to appear. Insight is a direct way of looking at what's going on within us, independent of discursive thought.

Hearing Steve express his frustration on the trail is a real bell of mindfulness. Suddenly, we're all invited to come back to the collective energy of walking on the earth. In the past, I notice, I might have gotten caught in my pride and reminded him we'd agreed to allow talking while walking after lunch, but I know that would only exacerbate his displeasure. So, after listening and pausing to breathe, I respond, "Yes, you're right. What does everyone think? Shall we continue to the hostel in silence so we can enjoy the forest?"

The group agrees with smiles, and we continue down the dirt track, now noticing the way it's interspersed with rounded stones and feeling lighter in our steps. Though simple, such moments remind me of the power of attention and the support of silence. They convince me over and over that mindfulness creates space and fertile soil not just for my own awakening, but for collective harmony.

Deep Listening and Silence
PHAP XA

In our tradition, we have a practice called Dharma Sharing. We sit in circles, whether in our monasteries, on retreat, or in the forest, and we practice deep listening together. One person speaks at a time, and the group holds space for them. There is no back-and-forth discussion or giving of advice unless it's explicitly asked for.

I have led Dharma Sharing groups for over twenty years, including on many hiking Zen retreats, and recently I had a rather unique experience: participants reacted against the format. While coleading a retreat for around forty Dutch speakers at the EIAB in Germany, I explained the format of Dharma Sharing in the usual way: we sit and offer our true presence to the person who is speaking; we listen without judging or interrupting the other person; we all speak from our own experience and do not comment or ask questions when others share. Dharma Sharing is a key practice that has proven itself to be profoundly healing and transformative in all our retreats; we can only listen deeply if we listen from a place of inner silence without the noise of our chattering mind.

After a round of introducing ourselves and talking about some of our difficulties, a woman new to our practices shared that this format, especially for her as a caregiver, was very difficult. She had just heard someone share painful feelings regarding the wars going on in the world, and no one had consoled the person who spoke—no hand on her shoulder, no verbal reaction, nothing. How could this bring healing? Two other men in the circle, also new to our center, then spoke up against the format as well. I was taken by surprise. In twenty years, I hadn't experienced anything like this. Was I going to say something? And what? I had already explained everything clearly, I thought.

I thought about how our group had moved to another room for our sharing circle and how on the way we had walked down a hallway of folk mosaics commissioned during the Nazi era. Right before the beginning of the Second World War, the building had been in the hands of the German Labor Front (Deutsche Arbeitsfront). By the end of the war, marble floors and stairways decorated a prestigious foyer and huge mosaics had been created on the wall. I imagined this heritage, protected by law, had affected the participants new to our center. Their discomfort had found its way into our Dharma Sharing circle.

Many of us carry the assumption that we are disconnected from each other. This makes us think that when we listen to pain and hurt expressed by others, that hurt is outside, not inside, of us. We therefore think we need to care for the pain outside, not inside, of ourselves. In our practice of Dharma Sharing, we are invited to stay connected to our bodies and hold a mindful space where we can collectively embrace this pain. It is a deep practice.

Another common assumption is that a wound needs to be healed immediately. In Zen, we are invited to first learn to accept and be with the wounds we carry. It is okay to suffer. Suffering has a role to play in our lives. We can learn and grow from it. This is connected to another common assumption: there is something wrong with unpleasant feelings. The format of Dharma Sharing challenges these assumptions, and that can be difficult to accept.

But Dharma Sharing can open a new possibility: Could it be that there is nothing wrong? Maybe it's just difficult for us to be with unpleasant feelings and emotions. Maybe that's okay. We can just sit, we can listen, we can help each other to be present for both the joys and the pains we experience without judging or reacting.

In the end, I chose to talk about my own challenges coping with the pain I experience in the world. I chose to share as a human rather than as someone caught in their role as the facilitator, more from the heart than from the head. I practiced speaking from a place of peace and freedom in myself rather than reacting, justifying, or defending. I knew this was just the first day of our retreat and trusted impermanence — things will change, and perhaps the healing power of silence will have time to unfold if people open themselves to it.

The next day, we decided to have Dharma Sharing all together in one big group. We began by singing together, and everyone benefited from a strong, collective energy of mindfulness that lit up the atmosphere. Song and spoken connection have their place together with thundering silence.

Walking Without Talking or Thinking

Walking without talking is a practice that reveals the power of *not* doing—the power of restraint. Refraining from action, including the act of thinking, is often the best way to turn an ordinary moment into a powerful moment of transformation. The mindfulness that arises helps us see both what to do *and* what not to do. Most of the doing in our lives doesn't come from a space of clarity. When we stop our incessant doing, we often learn that our best response in any situation may be to simply observe what's going on more deeply and expand our understanding. Our thinking can be the obstacle keeping us from truly enjoying the wonders of life within us and around us. If we master the practice of true presence, we can walk as a free person on the earth.

For this practice, find a quiet place with few distractions, outdoors if possible. Practice mindful walking as you've learned already; this time, with all your attention on your breath and your steps, notice each time you get pulled back into discursive thinking.

Be aware of when you get lost in daydreaming about the past or the future.

You may have the habit of trying to name or describe things you see in nature in the present moment, like the names of plants or animals. Every time your attention goes this way, gently guide it back to your breath and steps. You've done nothing wrong; you've just recognized a chance to deepen your mindfulness practice.

To make this practice easier, you may like to start with keywords, and then let the keywords fade from your mind as you enter a space of no thinking:

> *Breathing in, I take one or two steps. Breathing out, I take two or three steps.*
>
> *Breathing in: one, two. Breathing out: three, four, five.*
>
>> *One, two / Three, four, five.*
>> *In, in / Out, out, out.*

See if you can allow these keywords to fade into internal silence: no thinking, only walking. If you find yourself thinking again, go back to the first step and move again into a place of silence and non-thinking. This isn't a practice you're supposed to perform perfectly; it's a way of living and of walking gently. Be kind to yourself and allow the natural world to support you.

PRACTICE
Walking Together in True Silence

When you feel solid in the practice of not talking or thinking while walking, you may like to organize a group of people to meet and walk together in silence in nature. Establish the group intention of internal and external silence. You may like to start with just twenty or thirty minutes together. This is a powerful way to build community; without conversation, you become naturally more aware of everyone's presence in the group.

Here's how you can introduce the practice once the group is gathered:

> "We'll now practice walking meditation together. In walking meditation, we train ourselves to walk as free people on the earth. We combine our breathing with our steps so our mind is fully present in our bodies in this moment.
>
> For example, while breathing in we take one or two steps, and while breathing out we take two or three steps. Our out-breath may be longer than our in-breath.
>
> Whenever we get lost in thinking about the past, the future, or anything at all — tasks, worries — we gently guide our mind back to our breathing and the sensation of our steps on the earth.
>
> I'll lead the walk, so you don't need to think about where you're going. Let's stay together as a group to benefit from our shared mindfulness. From time to time, we may pause. If we do stop walking, just take a moment to fully enjoy the beauty of nature."

After the mindful walk in silence, you may like to sit together and reflect on the experience, if weather permits. Listen to each person speak about their experience of walking in silence. What came up? What was difficult? Was anything easy? What in their body and the surrounding landscape might they have observed for the first time?

If you like, it can be wonderful to integrate mindful walking in silence with a shared mindful meal afterward.

If you're leading a longer or faster walk in nature, such as a backpacking retreat or guided hike, you may take three or four steps on the in-breath and five or six steps on the out-breath. It's easier to start slower; there's no need to extend the breath unnaturally. Remember, we're re-training ourselves, developing a new habit of not rushing and not compulsively thinking while we walk. This takes time and is best done slowly. Practicing for just a few minutes each day will support your capacity to not think while walking. In time you may notice this skill of full presence helps you not to feed difficult emotions with your thinking when they inevitably arise.

Bringing It Home

How can you bring more silence—not talking or thinking—into your life? Consider creating analog spaces where you can disconnect from the internet and the unending stream of movies, music, and media and reconnect with yourself through silence. You can only listen deeply when you have enough silence within. Consider starting or ending each day with five to ten minutes of silent sitting, standing, lying, or walking. Even one minute built into your daily life can be a rich beginning. When you have enough silence, the thundering silence of the natural world can enter you: you can hear the trees and the animals speaking, you can hear the voice of your own heart.

CHAPTER SEVEN

Walking with Ancestors

Touching the Earth, Touching Our Roots

PHAP LUU

Donning our packs one morning in the early days of our seven-week trek, we set out in silence with the day's assigned practice in our hearts: walking with our ancestors. Stone walls meet at right angles along the rolling flank of the ridge we traverse on this section of the trail, a reminder of the pastures of the previous century. I imagine the descendants of the Dutch and English farmers — pioneers, hardy folk who braved the pass over the ridge — arriving here from the Hudson Valley in an exodus that destroyed both the old-growth forests and the lifeways of the Lenape peoples who had lived, breathed, and hunted amid these trees for centuries prior.

Where do our ancestors end? Our mother and father are in every cell of our body, along with their parents and countless generations before. But it doesn't stop here — our cells also include early hominid ancestors living chimpanzee-like in the canopy of a jungle; they include a burrowing mammal who reared its young underground, out of sight and scent of land-roving predators; a therapsid, the reptilian ancestor of all mammals, who basked in the sun on four legs long before flowers and grasses existed and guarded its hard-shell eggs in a nest; an amphibian-like creature who fed on insects on land but scurried, salamander-like, on stubby legs and belly to briny waters to lay soft eggs. Our cells even include the fish who began occasionally to push up with its front fins from the mud of the water's shallows to breathe the air—how novel![7] I'm in awe of all these ancestors in and with us in the present moment as we, now upright on two legs tread mindfully along the trail.

I return to the sensation of the earth beneath my feet as we wind our way on soft forest paths toward the border of modern-day New York-New Jersey. Moving together like a caterpillar, a few of us carry walking sticks to balance ourselves and to flick away fallen branches from spring storms. At a brook I drop my pack and move upstream, hopping from rock to dirt knoll until I find a pulse where water comes clean out of the earth. Taking close note of the natural spring and low risk of contamination, I put my lips directly to the cool water as it emerges from the ground.

How strange our human notion of a self suddenly seems! Truly, a flowing stream of ancestors courses through this body that I call mine, a river converges and continues like the water flowing into my mouth. Who can say which bit of the Delaware River is now this spring, cold on my lips? How could I section off some part of this body and mind to say *that is Grandpa Bachman, the hunter, the boat-seller, the entrepreneur*; *this is Grandpa Rice, the salesman, moving from job to job, never settled*; *this is Grandma Bachman, stern, quiet, practical, romantic, and good with numbers*; *this is Grandma Rice, diligent, prolific, always ready to lend money?* All these parts flow together in and through this body, just as the spring water between my lips is also the liquid pulsing through my veins.

I never knew my father's father. When I think of him, I often recall the story of the 1955 flood in Waterbury, Connecticut. "It rained heavily on the 18th of August as the second hurricane in a week passed nearby," my father told me. He had been thirteen at the time, living with his parents and three younger sisters in the apartment above the main showroom of the marine business my grandfather ran, which sold mostly boats and outboard motors.

A loud knock on the front door at 3:00 a.m. woke the family. My father peeked through the window to see the parking lot filled with police cars, fire trucks, and ambulances. At the door, a police officer shared an order to commandeer all my grandfather's boats. Floodwaters from the Naugatuck River had already taken lives and were threatening more in nearby Waterbury. Over the next twelve hours, my grandfather risked his own life with multiple trips through raging flood water in a boat powered by a twenty-five-horsepower Evinrude—the most powerful outboard available then—to rescue people trapped in the upper stories of threatened buildings. My grandfather left my father behind after seeing the extent of the risk he faced. He managed to keep his boat running through dangerous standing waves when others broke down, and he got dozens of people out of buildings that were later swept away.

Reflecting on my grandfather's selfless actions has helped me establish a connection to a blood ancestor I never had a chance to meet. When I touch elements of courage and nonself in me, I know I'm touching my grandfather. Of course, like everyone, I surely have numerous blood ancestors who acted in harmful, cowardly, or selfish ways. I've done so myself. Yet without ignoring the painful legacies or the intergenerational healing I can offer my family and myself with my mindful presence, the moments when people rose above fear or small-mindedness to act with courageous kindness inspire me to continue wholeheartedly.

Descending the trail from southern New York into what must be New Jersey after drinking from that eternally flowing spring, I draw deep sustenance from feeling my ancestors walking within me, alongside me, behind me. The trail leads to a cool, dark series of wide paths and boardwalks sheltered by the huge leaves of intricate, spreading branches. Bits of snow remain in the shadiest spots and cool streams flow lazily through thawed mud. A rise on a ridge gives us a view of the ancient Lenape homeland to the east as our group of biped hikers emerges on the slope of High Point—we and all our ancestors.

As our Appalachian Trail retreat continues, we return each week to this ancestor awareness practice. Two hundred fifty miles later, we're walking with our ancestors in Maryland, moving through cool fog and light drizzle, when a close-cropped field opens before us. On the crest of a hill is a remarkable circular stone structure, over thirty feet high and narrowing into a double ring at its top. As we approach, its form and mass emerge from the mist. I note its locked iron gate—entrance to the internally ascending stairway is barred. This, we realize, must be the first Washington Monument, erected mostly in a day—July 4, 1827—in a passion of patriotism by most of the five hundred inhabitants of nearby Boonsboro. The tower is dry-laid from carefully cut blocks of adjacent blue rock granite outcroppings and has been restored twice—once after the Civil War, and once by the Civilian Conservation Corps in the 1930s after time and neglect rendered it ruined rubble. Its uncanny resemblance to a stupa—a monument erected to house sacred remains of the Buddha or his disciples and a place for meditation—surprises me.

As a novice monk in Plum Village, France, every Saturday afternoon I used to practice "Touching the Earth" with the community. At the sound of the bell, we knelt until our limbs were folded on the ground and our upper body prostrate, our palms facing upward and our foreheads resting on the earth. Here we paused, aware of our breathing, and listened to a text read aloud for contemplation. After practicing in this way many times, I remember the lines well:

> *I see myself touching the land ancestors of Indigenous origin, who have lived on this land for such a long time and known the ways to live in peace and harmony with nature, protecting the mountains, forests, animals, vegetation, and minerals of this land. I feel the energy of this land penetrating my body and soul, supporting and accepting me. I vow to cultivate and maintain this energy and transmit it to future generations. I vow to contribute my part to transforming the violence, hatred, and delusion that still lie deep in the collective consciousness of this society so future generations will have more safety, joy, and peace. I thank this land for its protection and support.*

Looking up at the first Washington Monument, its nondescript granite appears sinister in the fog — the parapet at the top takes on the form of a battlement in my imagination, the closed iron gate that of the entrance to a dungeon. I stand with feelings of wonder mixed with regret. The arrival of Europeans — uninvited — on this continent has left us with a huge legacy of devastation. It's no wonder so many of us have become paralyzed, often unable to offer gratitude or connect to our ancestors.

Zen speaks of the middle way, the way between extremes, as the way of wisdom and freedom. The middle way means, on the one hand, not being blind to the harm done by our ancestors and, on the other, acknowledging and cultivating gratitude for our roots. Standing with my feet firmly on the earth, facing the stone tower, I feel myself beset with the contradictions of my ancestry—Catholic, Protestant, conservative, progressive, right, left, perpetrator, victim, all of it in me—and come back to my breathing. The breath is here. That's enough. It's only in the present, with presence, that we can find our way to move skillfully into a future of healing and justice.

Saving *Onderduikers*

PHAP XA

Setting foot on the grounds of Blue Cliff Monastery at the start of our Appalachian Trail retreat brought back many memories. In August 2007, I had traveled with Thay to the United States on a one-way ticket. As a monk, I'm committed to doing what is determined to be best for the community; I have let go of deciding for myself, based purely on my own interests. In this case, that meant I'd be staying on as a resident at Blue Cliff after the mindfulness retreat Thay was to lead there.

Blue Cliff is ensconced in a forest of hemlock fir and beech with wild rhododendrons clustered in small, scattered bogs. When the first monks and nuns moved in, they discovered deer paths crisscrossing the landscape and quickly began widening them as walking meditation trails, working with mindful steps and a commitment to minimal clearing. During my time at Blue Cliff, I very much enjoyed walking the four-mile loop around the neighborhood, sometimes accompanied by other brothers and sisters and sometimes on my own. I also recall many hours spent in the forest with a chainsaw, searching for downed wood to cut up and leave to cure for future winter fires in the monks' residence.

These happy memories of being outdoors at Blue Cliff echo those from my childhood. It's always been a joy for me to be active outside. Growing up on a farm in the Eastern Netherlands, not far from the German border, I was accustomed to outdoor work, to breathing fresh air charged with the scent of turned soil. I often worked on the tractor, sometimes spending the whole day riding around mowing or removing cut grass to compress and save for the winter to feed the milk cows. Since so many of my activities were far away from our farm—school, friends, soccer practice—I often traveled from place to place on my bike. High school in the city of Arnhem, about ten miles away, meant one hour of riding on the flat Dutch bicycle paths that flanked the main road.

My father inherited the farm from his father; I was part of the sixth generation of our family to live there. I'd heard stories about my paternal grandparents, but they both died before I was born. My grandfather was shot during the World War II Nazi occupation of the Netherlands from 1940 to 1945, and my grandmother passed away soon after my parents married. During the occupation, our farm was a refuge for "onderduikers"—people hiding from the Nazi German army. *Onderduiker* literally means "under diver" and describes people who went into hiding, especially to escape persecution or forced labor by the Nazi regime, during World War II. During this time, I'd been told, families and some single men stayed on our farm—among them a Nazi deserter.

Times were dangerous, and my grandparents were anxious about our family's safety. Though I never heard much about it from my father, a young man named Simon who had stayed at the farm later wrote a detailed narrative about his war experiences. From his story, I learned that one morning, a Dutch onderduiker decided to try his luck and move on. He disguised himself in a Nazi Wehrmacht uniform, grabbed a rifle and some hand grenades, and headed down the road. Later that day, he was arrested. Right away his mother rushed to the farm and warned all the men to flee; she felt sure her son would talk under the pressure of interrogation. Simon advised my grandfather to hide; any men present when the Gestapo arrived would surely be detained. My grandfather, standing out on the field beside the farm when he heard the news, followed his first thought and returned to the house to protect his family. His noble action had dire consequences, though. On Christmas Eve, 1944, he was arrested.

A few months later, on the night of March 6, 1945, some members of the Dutch resistance disguised themselves in German uniforms to ambush a Nazi truck. The BMW motorcar they ended up stopping carried the highest German SS officer in the Netherlands, Hanns Rauters. The resistance fighters shot all the Germans in the motorcar, but Rauters feigned death and survived. As a reprisal for this attack, on March 8, 1945, the occupying German forces executed 117 political prisoners. My grandfather was one of those prisoners. He was forty-eight at the time, my father only eleven.

In his narrative account of the war, Simon described my grandparents as "such good people, who never thought of themselves and were always ready to help others."[8] When I read this sentence, it made me deeply happy. Despite my lack of interest in taking over what had been their farm, I saw that my grandparents and I had remarkably similar aspirations. In vastly different circumstances, we turned and turn toward helping others. I continue their aspiration in my own life—though in a different form as a Zen monk—offering people a place of refuge and dedicating myself to helping transform their suffering.

The day I returned to Blue Cliff for our mindful hiking retreat (I hadn't lived there for eight years by that time), I took a walk in the forest by myself. It was early morning, and I noticed the imperfection of my memories. The shape and length of the paths I'd traversed so often in my mind didn't match what was on the ground beneath me. The exact location and shape of Moon Lake was far different from what I remembered. Contemplating the lives and aspirations of my ancestors is a core part of my practice. Walking on the land of Blue Cliff again, I visualized my long-dead grandfather and the two grandmothers I'd never known walking alongside me. The little bits I knew of them and the pictures I'd seen surfaced in my mind, and I smiled to them and saw them smiling back at me. We walked together.

Saying, "These grandparents have passed away" is part of the truth. Yet Zen has shown me it's also true that my grandparents are still alive in me, in every cell of my body. Their DNA, their experiences, their joy, and their suffering continue in me. This is also true. There's an everyday reality, and there's a reality that transcends the boundaries of birth and death. It doesn't have to be one or the other.

Walking with my grandparents in the forest of Blue Cliff, I also walked *for* them. My grandparents, like everyone who has ever lived, had their difficulties and their suffering; walking with them in mindfulness and care, their lives, joys, and hardships continued in me. My practice is to cultivate happiness and transform my suffering, which is connected to, not different from, their suffering. In Zen, it's said that becoming a monk or a nun and having the chance to deeply transform the roots of suffering is a great fortune, a fortune you receive thanks to the work of your ancestors. As monks, we're reminded that we'll never be able to pay this gratitude we owe. In fact, the Buddhist sutras say you wouldn't be able to repay this ancestral debt even if you carried your father on one shoulder and your mother on the other for the whole of your life!

Some may think to be happy or to cultivate happiness is selfish when there's so much suffering in the world. But to me it's clear: If you're not happy, how can you contribute to the happiness of others? Thay liked to use the analogy of swimming—only if you know how to swim can you save yourself and others from drowning. Likewise, only if you know how to transform your own suffering—which includes the suffering of your ancestors—into happiness and peace can you help others not to drown in their own misery. This insight inspires me to be happy for myself, my parents, my grandparents, and the world.

On Ancestors

For better or for worse, our ancestors are in us—their fears and their heroism, their joys and their pains. Walking with them in awareness can be a deeply healing practice, even (or especially) if this means walking with the pain we feel they've inflicted on us. In understanding our connection to them and the complexity of each life, we can let go of resentment and begin to nourish ourselves with the harvest of generations of wisdom.

It's easy to see that a cloud is another form of the water vapor that came off the ocean or a lake and that the cloud will transform into rain or snow and fill the rivers and lakes of our planet. We wouldn't think for a moment that the cloud is separate from the vapor, the rain, the river, or the ocean. Similarly, when we look deeply, we can see our body and mind are part of a stream containing our ancestors and descendants. We become free of the limited, narrow view that we are separate individuals.

Practicing with our ancestors is deep, powerful work. When we offer walking with our ancestors as a practice on our mindful hiking retreats after a few days focused on mindful breathing and walking, it always brings up tears for some—an emotional release. Though deeply supportive of (and perhaps even necessary for) transformation and healing, connecting with the realities of our ancestors' lives and the ways they've impacted us can be an intense experience.

One retreat participant, George M., experienced reconnection with his Taíno ancestors. He tells the story best: "I spent twenty years in the Marines and many years in recovery, and in the past two years have experienced considerable difficulties: the loss of my older brother, a seventeen-year romantic relationship ending, and brain surgery for an aneurysm. I have been a hiker and marathon runner for many years and my mentality was frequently to attack the hill. Our hiking retreats have changed the way I look at things. My walking now is mostly mindful walking; I practice mindfulness and staying in the present moment, where I often experience a sense of peace and increased awareness. For the last twenty years, I have returned to my native teachings through honoring the earth—I participate in the *inipe* ceremony frequently called 'sweat lodge' to connect with my elders and previous generations. The practice of walking with the ancestors has brought me closer to these previous generations in me. I generally no longer walk as if I have a mission to accomplish but to be peaceful in the moment."

Another mindful hiking retreatant had recently discovered she was born as a result of her father raping her mother. Having time outside to walk with her ancestors in mindfulness while experiencing the support of the natural world helped her to integrate this painful knowledge. She shares:

"One morning during our mindful backpacking retreat in the Sierra Nevada Mountains, I learned that the day's practice would be walking with our ancestors. As I listened to the monastics share how we are all interconnected through the earth—that our bodies ultimately integrate with the soil, transforming into the very essence of nature itself—I began to observe the beauty of the surrounding forest with fresh eyes. A pinecone fell beside me, and I thought about its life cycle: how it would decompose in the soil, enrich the earth, and grow into a tall tree, representing the legacy of the ancestors that had come before it. Up to this point, I had sometimes come across meditations focused on ancestors; separated by my own individualistic upbringing in America, I had simply scrolled past them. Standing in the embrace of the Sierra wilderness, I knew it was time to confront this topic.

"After enjoying breakfast and packing our things, we began our hike. Walking in contemplative silence, I gazed up at towering sequoia and pine trees and thought about their longevity and resilience—the many seasons they had seen, the multitudes of creatures, human and non-human, who had been here before me, and the innumerable storms and fires they had survived. Each tree seemed an embodiment of many ancestors, and my thoughts naturally drifted to my own ancestral connections.

"I feel a profound closeness to my mother's family; it's easy for me to honor their journeys of courage and compassion. They fought for vulnerable populations even when it was unpopular, transcended societal limitations to achieve their dreams, and were guided by spirituality. Reflecting on their strength filled me with warmth and joy. Yet as we continued walking, space opened for more. Having never met my biological father, I only know him through stories that make me feel shame and fear: I know he is in prison. My mother recently informed me I am a product of rape. This painful fact has been hard to accept.

"As I walked amid the trees, I began to ruminate: if I am interconnected with my ancestors and embody their energy, I must also carry the weight of my father's actions within me. Tears filled my eyes as I envisioned his violent, self-seeking energy and recognized the objectification and powerlessness my mother must have felt.

"When we stopped for our Dharma circle, I shared through tears about my morning. I felt strength and safety in the sangha; my vulnerability was met with the compassionate embrace of the group. This nurturing environment allowed me to safely unpack the heavy thoughts and emotions that surfaced and the remainder of that day became a journey of acceptance. I spent the afternoon witnessing the unfolding emotions and thoughts in my body and mind. The simplicity of walking through nature became an anchor, providing me the necessary space to face the powerful topic of my ancestors.

"It is essential to embrace and accept all facets of ourselves; walking in nature with others provides the grounding strength to do so. Just as the earth accepts, integrates, and transforms, so too can I. The afflictions and traumas of my ancestors can be transmuted through me. Walking with our ancestors in nature not only allows us to confront our shadows but also illuminates the path to healing, acceptance, and love for all parts of ourselves."

Both of these powerful sharings reveal how spending an entire day walking with blood ancestors allowed compassion to emerge and healing to take place. How can we expect to get along with each other in the present moment if our ancestors, all that is inside of us, can't be in peace? Each of us, with our ancestors, needs to practice peace for peace on Earth to be possible.

PRACTICE

Walk with Your Ancestors

What follows is one example of walking with a specific ancestor; you can replace "grandma" in the following with grandpa, mom, dad, or any other ancestor — blood, spirit, or land. It's not only the humans and living creatures we come from who form us and walk with us. We are also formed by the places, teachers, and companions we've known and leaned on in our lives.

Be honest with yourself about whether this practice is supportive and appropriate for you right now. Finding someone or a group of people to explore this work with can be very helpful. If you'd like to explore this practice, take a moment — ideally outdoors to draw on the support of the natural world — to stand with solidity on the earth and notice the air around you becoming the breath moving in and out of your body. Feel the stability of the ground beneath your feet.

At any moment, you can practice walking with your ancestors. Choose one: it may be a beloved grandmother or father. Knowing the cells of your body are a continuation of theirs, take their hand. It's easy to do this; their cells are already in your hand.

Slowly begin to walk when you feel ready, bringing the following phrases to mind as you stay connected to your breath.

> *Breathing in: Grandma, I walk with you. Breathing out: I know you're there in each step.*

*Walking with grandma / Grandma present in
each step.*

*Breathing in: I enjoy the wonders of the present moment
with you, grandma. Breathing out: This is a wonderful
moment.*

Present moment / Wonderful moment.

*Breathing in: I'm aware of the suffering you couldn't
transform. Breathing out: I let that suffering flow
through me into the earth.*

*Aware of Grandma's suffering / Letting the
suffering flow into the Earth.*

*Breathing in: I kiss the earth with the soles of my feet.
Breathing out: Together we walk lightly on the earth.*

Feet kissing the earth / Walking lightly on the earth.

*Breathing in: I let the whole stream of ancestors walk
with me on the Earth. Breathing out: I transmit this
energy of mindfulness to all my ancestors.*

*Stream of ancestors walking / Transmitting mind-
fulness to ancestors.*

*Breathing in: We walk together in peace on the earth.
Breathing out: Peace is the walking.*

We walk in peace / Peace is walking.

This practice of walking with our ancestors is a deep
one. During their lives, our ancestors may not have had

the opportunity to walk mindfully on the earth. Now, we can help them transform their suffering and fear. It is joyful to do this practice together with others. When we walk together and we see all our ancestors walking with us, our walking meditation contains unimaginably vast multitudes, present in every cell of our body. On our hiking retreats, this means thousands of us walk together—a true peace walk.

Bringing It Home

When we know our blood ancestors continue in the present moment in every cell of our body, we see we are not alone in our transformation and healing. This can give us an enormous amount of energy to go deeper into our practice of mindfulness: we practice together with our ancestors and have all their resources available to us. They may not have had the chance to learn about mindfulness, but now that we have this precious practice, we can commit with them to transform the unhealed intergenerational trauma, pain, and anxiety they have transmitted to us.

Consider setting aside five to ten minutes each week for walking with your blood ancestors. Though this can be an intense emotional practice you may prefer to do together with others in community or on your own in a private place, it's also something you can do as you walk anywhere—around the block with your dog, from your car to the post office, or even on your way to the bathroom. Experiment for yourself. Bit by bit, healing can begin to take place.

CHAPTER EIGHT

Healing Is in Your Nature

A Mindful Lunch on the Appalachian Trail

PHAP LUU

Rain falls as we descend from the crest of South Mountain in Maryland. A side trail to Pine Knob shelter branches off to the north. Dreaming of a dry space to drop our gear and eat lunch, we happily make our way toward the shelter. When we arrive, a bearded man in his thirties is comfortably leaning against the back wall, dry amid his worn mat and gear. His eyes widen at the sight of a brown-robed, bald figure leading a bunch of silent hikers in his direction.

"I'm taking the day off to stay out of the rain," he drawls. Out on the trail, even city dwellers from the urban sprawl of New England tend to acquire a backcountry, relaxed mode of speech—their own Appalachian Trail dialect. I've noticed it more and more as we move south into the wave of hikers trekking north from Mt. Springer in Georgia.

"Who're you folks?" he asks.

We share that we're on a mindful hiking retreat, hoping to connect to ourselves and the earth with the support of age-old Zen practices.

"Don't mind me. I've already eaten. Please, you're welcome," he declares when we ask if he wants to join us for lunch.

We've been following the same guidelines at meals as are practiced in Zen centers and monasteries around the world. So, I take out the small bell I carry in my backpack and invite its sound three times once everyone is seated in a dry place with their lunch in front of them. Each bright sound is an invitation for us to take a moment to come back to our bodies, our breath, and our senses. After we've paused to follow the bell's ringing into silence, I offer a recitation of the Five Contemplations. Though the wording varies slightly among Zen traditions, these contemplations focus on awareness of where our food comes from, acknowledgment of all that it contains, and gratitude for the sustenance that allows us to continue walking the path of mindfulness and awakening. We then eat in silence for about fifteen minutes, our bearded friend looking on in wonder.

The collective energy of mindfulness generated when people practice together has its own power, a power that goes far beyond what any one person can create by themselves. When people practice together, a wave of peace, openness, and compassion ripples out to include others. This is why, over the years, groups of meditators have gathered in places like the UN Climate Change Conference, outside of diplomatic institutions, or the areas surrounding peace negotiations. It sounds mystical, but I've seen the profound effect of collective mindfulness. When Thay was in a coma after his stroke in 2014, the calm mindfulness of the monastic disciples who cared for him 24/7 in the intensive care unit of the hospital in Bordeaux created a space of refuge for doctors and nurses overwhelmed with the daily stress of being with the dying. Again and again, health care workers told us they looked forward to being in the room with Thay; it refreshed them, it even brought joy. Thay and those he taught contributed peace even when he was in a coma!

Our meal eaten, I close the silence with two more sounds of the bell. As the last waves of sound recede, our new friend exclaims, "Well, I've never experienced anything quite like that before!" A broad grin on his face, he begins to pepper us with questions. Hikers on the Appalachian Trail are often questioning their purpose in life, hoping to find answers by putting one foot in front of the other out in nature. This wasn't the first or last time a fellow hiker wanted to understand more about our practice and how it corresponds with the healing they're seeking on the trail.

Transmitting such collective energy by surprise to hikers we meet along the Appalachian Trail, as happened that day in Pine Knob shelter, was a never-ending source of joy for us. Zen or not, clothed in monastic brown robes or synthetic hiking gear, all of us are inevitably changed when we spend days on end walking mindfully through the forest.

Connecting with Zen

PHAP XA

I grew up feeling very much at home on our family farm in the Netherlands. The summer holidays were especially dear to me—we had time to play. As children, my best friend, Marcel, and I played every day: soccer, tennis, squash. We ran together, watched movies together; we even enjoyed the heavy work on the farm like collecting bales of hay out on the field. I remember often feeling very content.

When it came time to go to university, I was happy to move out of the house and start a new life. After briefly considering studying medicine, I settled on applied mathematics and headed to Enschede, a nearby city. Suddenly, my life became much more complicated. I didn't know anyone, and no one knew me. No longer living with my family, a whole new level of freedom opened; at first, I only saw advantages.

It turned out I was more interested in building a social life than in studying. Thursday evenings were student evenings in town; many bars and restaurants offered special deals, and Saturday nights were local evenings. On Friday morning, the last bars closed at 4:00 a.m.; I usually went to bed after that, around 5:00 a.m. Two hours later, at 7:00 a.m., I'd get up for my 8:30 lecture, too sleepy and hungover to learn anything.

As much as I enjoyed my dynamic social life—going out, playing pool, and drinking—I became increasingly aware of some sort of wound deep inside. It became more and more tangible until it no longer ever completely disappeared. Being around others soothed the pain temporarily, but it always found a way to the surface.

I started keeping a diary. Words came easily, even if I was tired at 2:00 a.m. I experienced so many emotions, joys, and frustrations that writing them down became a deep need. In that first year of university, quite a bit of pain came up. I didn't know where it came from, and I didn't know what to do with it. The diary helped, and toward the end of the year, I found another way of dealing with the pain—I focused on studying. Then, I began spontaneously sitting quietly for fifteen minutes every day, just doing nothing. I discovered "aimlessness," which I would later learn is a pillar of freedom and healing in Zen. Those fifteen minutes of space each day began to open something in me.

I decided to respond to an invitation I'd seen several times in the university newspaper: "Zen Meditation, Thursdays, 7–9 p.m." The next Thursday evening, I parked my bike in front of an old, narrow building downtown. Rein, a gray-haired man in his fifties, opened the door and invited me inside. Right away I noticed his joyful yet down-to-earth manner. Upstairs, Andre and Bert drank tea around a table, a pleasant change from the cold, wet winter I'd left outside.

Soon we moved into an L-shaped attic where a handful of people already sat facing the wall. In classic Zen meditation, I learned, it's customary to limit distractions by sitting in front of a blank wall. The meditation went on and on, the experience totally new to me. I wasn't supposed to pay attention to what the others were doing, but I couldn't help it. Rein sat like a rock. I had the impression I sat and shifted around on my cushion for much longer than thirty minutes, but in fact, I later learned it had been less—out of consideration for me, the newcomer, our sit had lasted only twenty-five minutes.

After a bell sounded, everyone stood for a short practice of walking meditation. We passed by each other quite closely in the narrow attic, but no one made eye contact or spoke. The pleasant fragrance of incense, the dim light of candles, the silence, the sitting still—all of it was both intriguing and strange.

I wasn't sure quite what to think, but I kept returning. I became very enthusiastic about Zen and started to sit every morning at home; I joined a second Zen group that met on Monday evenings to sit silently for four or five periods of thirty-five minutes each. In silent meditation, the turmoil in my heart eased. I experienced deep peace and stillness—more than I had ever felt in my life. This was enough to get me hooked. Though we sat in silence, the presence of others was palpable.

Somehow, our unspoken connection supported my practice; sensing that it was deeply human to yearn for peace and joy eased my feelings of isolation.

When I discovered a book by Thich Nhat Hanh at the public library, my understanding of Zen expanded. In contrast to other books I'd read, Thay's book proved very practical; it didn't just apply to sitting on my cushion, but to my whole life. Eventually I read *Old Path White Clouds*, Thay's retelling of the life of the Buddha. This book deeply inspired me; insight into how the Buddha reached such a deep level of concentration felt like a profound window into the human mind. More and more, a sense of shared humanity pulled me forward toward the healing I knew was possible.

On Interbeing

As Zen practitioners, we see ourselves not as single drops of water, but as a river flowing together with all of humanity, all living beings, and all that is. Sometimes something in us doesn't want to let ourselves flow with the river—we want to be an individual; we don't want to adapt to the conditions of our social group or community. Maybe we want the community to adapt to our own ideas and needs. But flowing like a river, harmonizing our views with those around us, supports the happiness of the whole community, whether that's a group of friends backpacking, a family, or a monastery.

Though we tend to see ourselves as separate and distinct from other humans, animals, plants, and minerals, an ancient

Buddhist text called the Diamond Sutra, one of the earliest texts on deep ecology, teaches us not to get trapped by views based on the concept of a self, a person, a living being, or a lifespan. Such views cause us to separate ourselves from the rest of the phenomenal world, an ignorance which feeds emotions like despair, fear, and anxiety in ourselves and in others.

When we learn to let go of these views, we no longer entertain ideas about me, mine, or myself, and we flow naturally with the river of all phenomena. As Thay often reminded us, we can see the cloud in our tea and the tea in ourselves— without the cloud that carries the rain that falls on plants in the field, the tea in our cup could not exist. Without the liquid in our bodies, we would dry up and blow away—our cells are literally made of everything we consume, from the food in our bellies to the air in our lungs. This is the insight of interbeing.

What does this mean in everyday life? Well, when we enter a wild space, such as the forest, on a long walk with others, the main purpose is to practice being together, to walk together as one, and to be happy. Walking in wildness, we can let go of our fixed ideas and notions and simply enjoy the presence of the community around us. A river doesn't need any leader, it just flows according to gravity. In a true community the same is true. When we learn to take refuge in our community, we naturally flow in the direction of love and understanding. We don't need anyone to direct us.

If we're walking alone, we can still see ourselves as part of a stream of life—one with the trees, the plants, the animals, and the minerals in and around us. We're not a drop of water cut off from the river. We're deeply connected to the river, to the whole stream of life. We are never truly alone.

PRACTICE
Eating Meditation

Prepare a delicious, simple, and healthy picnic—vegetarian or entirely plant-based—with fresh fruit and hot water for tea. In Zen we see the act of consuming food as medicinal—this includes both the food itself and the way we eat it. Go to a beautiful place in nature near you, a park, field, or forest, for example—or even your backyard. If you're on a hiking trip, pick one of your daily meals for this practice.

Once you've arrived, set the food on the ground in front of you, on a cloth if you like. Sit down and come back to your breathing. Notice where your body is in contact with the earth beneath you. Make sure you take the time to allow peace to arise. It's important to wait until you feel relaxed before you begin eating. If you eat while stressed, angry, or impatient, you will consume those feelings along with your food. The food and the way we eat it both impact our well-being.

Now, look at the food laid out before you. Look deeply. This food and your body inter-are. The food in front of you, like all food, grew with the help of the sun, the rain, the soil, the farmer who tended it. And it only lies before you thanks to the driver who transported it, and the many other beings who made it possible for you to have this nourishment. You may even be preparing to eat some food you've grown yourself! Either way, pause for a moment and silently express gratitude for the work and the people that brought you this food.

Aware of your breathing, now look deeply into your own body. Your body is made of food. It comes from your parents, from the food they ate, and from the food you eat—from the sun, the rain, and the soil. Your body may be in good health; if so, give silent thanks for this condition and the happiness it brings.

You may like to recite—to yourself or aloud—the Five Contemplations:

1. This food is a gift of the earth, the sky, numerous living beings, and much hard and loving work.

2. May we eat with mindfulness and gratitude to be worthy of it.

3. May we recognize and transform unwholesome mental formations, especially our greed, and learn to eat in moderation.

4. May we keep our compassion alive by eating in a way that reduces the suffering of living beings, stops contributing to climate change, and heals and preserves our precious planet.

5. We accept this food to nourish our siblinghood, build our community, and realize our ideal of serving all living beings.

Now eat in silence. Eat slowly, noting the taste and texture of each bite. This is a wondrous reunion! The food and you, born of the sun, the rain, and the earth, come together in this moment. You are a part, not apart. While you eat, pause to look around. Notice the elements surrounding you, also present in your food and in your body. Eating in nature can create a powerful experience of interbeing, of seeing that we're not separate from the environment — that we ourselves are the environment. Notice if you can feel the truth of this insight, allow it to unfold, and see where it leads you.

To develop this practice further, you may like to put down your spoon, fork, or chopsticks as you chew each morsel twenty or thirty times before swallowing. That way you can focus completely on the experience of food in your mouth, not multitasking by preparing to take the next bite even as you chew and swallow.

Bringing It Home

How do you practice interbeing in your daily life? If you look deeply at something, you can see it connected to many other things. When you look at a prisoner, for example, you can also see the society and conditions they grew up in that contributed (along with personal choice) to making them into someone who commits a crime. Notice where you draw lines and categories in your thinking and actions: friend and enemy, left and right, good and bad. Perhaps take a few notes as instances occur to you.

With this awareness, bring to mind someone you consider a type of enemy. Can you make them a friend by realizing they can help you to understand yourself more deeply? Perhaps you're able to recognize a positive quality or two your so-called enemy might have, even if these don't erase the difficulty they represent to you.

When you look at your enemy in this way, you can see much more than just a difficult person.

Notice in your daily life how often you sit with someone who is on the other side of any issue. Can you commit to learning such a person's deepest aspirations? You don't have to condone their actions or beliefs, but can you incline your awareness toward a willingness to relate to and understand those around you?

Interbeing isn't a theory, it's a practice. When we make it a part of our daily life, we start to include everything—people, animals, plants, and minerals—as part of our sphere of experience. Our life becomes whole.

CHAPTER NINE

The Path of Action

Building Trails, Building Community

PHAP LUU

As a monk, I've built numerous trails at Deer Park Monastery in Escondido, California, and each one has been a revelation. Each one teaches me something new about the difficulties and joys of the spiritual path. In many ways, the spiritual path is not a metaphor. It can be the physical path we walk—whether a new path we clear in the chaparral, a trail we traverse in the forest, or the mindful steps we take on concrete. The path is liberative because of the nature of our steps.

Trail building can be a mindful art. The Buddha himself was a trailblazer, opening an ancient path he called the Dharma. As a young boy, I distinctly remember building my first trail, something I could do on the largely wild, forested hillside our house perched upon. When I was about twelve, my father dedicated the whole week of my spring break to the project of building a tree house at the bottom of the hill in our Connecticut backyard together. We recycled wood from our old dock to use for siding and bolted two beams across the cleared surface of two pine trunks. An old window from our house's construction a decade before provided a view of the lake below—a lake created by a dam on the Housatonic River built in the aftermath of the 1955 flood I mentioned above. My father designed an ingenious ladder that could be lowered via a pulley and rope going through the floor to become a staircase as part of the uphill wall of the tree house. When we finished, I spent one cold night out there—scary, but unforgettable.

To get straight down to the tree house from our house up the hill, I cleared a secret path that started right below a series of jagged rocks where my sister, cousin, and I used to pretend to crew the Battlestar *Galactica*. The path was steep, and I didn't add any switchbacks, yet the skills I learned building it—clearing brush, eyeing the lay of the land for good footing, noticing which spaces (maybe where deer or coyote had travelled) invited passage—still inform my path building today.

A core principle of path building is to do minimal harm. You don't fight with the terrain; instead, you enter a profound flow state in which the path suggests itself. I do cut branches, move rocks, and sometimes extirpate a bush. This is painful for the plant and the living beings who depend on it. But I learn to minimize the harm, to back up frequently and rethink the trajectory of the path. Trail building, I've learned, is an intimate art of observation and implementation. At every moment, you must stop, reassess, adapt a new plan, and then act. Can I leave that bush intact? Are there many other plants of that type, and will it sprout up again easily in this ecosystem? Some places speak to you, saying: Don't touch. I can't explain this process entirely. You see a large, green scorpion, or notice that a rattlesnake makes an area its lair, and you know to leave it alone. Poison oak? You can pull it out at the root, but beware. It may come back to haunt you. At Deer Park Monastery, poison oak is a native plant. Who am I to wage war against it?

When you become skilled in the art of path building, most of what you clear away will be dead matter. You learn to observe the landscape in your mind to know where the best footing is. You know when to go around, when to find another way, and when to continue straight ahead. Walking established paths, as we did most of the time during our seven weeks on the Appalachian Trail, connects you with those who have come before and created the path. There is love in a trail.

All this holds true for the spiritual path. I've certainly made mistakes and done harm without realizing it. But trail building taught me: stop before you inflict a wound carelessly—by word or deed—and back up. Look around, see if there's another way. Remember the path is the destination—the experience is the walking, and by walking you build the path. Walk mindfully, and others will enjoy their own steps on the path you contribute to. Focus on the experience of building the path. When the building and the walking become one, you integrate the spiritual path, the path of the mind, and the path you walk on: mind and body unite. There's only the path and the walking—no path maker, no walker. We already are what we want to become. The path reveals itself with each step.

The Winding Path to Ordination

PHAP XA

As a child, like many, I thought I was special. I thought I was the center of the universe and everything revolved around me. I even thought I came from another planet; I had no idea why I was on Planet Earth. But it wasn't so much that I believed I was special as that I really wanted to *be* special. The collective consciousness of society—especially what I saw on TV—watered these seeds in me, and I wanted to be famous, rich, popular, healthy, and sexy. The "how" wasn't so important. I could be a soccer star, a world-class tennis player, or a kind of Bill Gates.

When I decided to become a monk, I traded these goals for the path of transformation and healing. The discovery of Zen meditation was like finding a precious gem. In it, I recognized what I really longed for: peace and inner stillness. Arriving in Plum Village, the practice center where I became a monk, was like coming home. My first opportunity to visit Plum Village, the monastery described in Thay's books, came at the end of 2000. I'd participated in Zen sesshins—intensive meditation retreats in the Japanese Zen tradition—in the Netherlands, but the winter retreat in Plum Village was completely different. The people there—resident monks and nuns who committed their lives to Zen practice as well as lay people committed to staying for several months or years—inspired me from the start. In the sesshins I'd attended, as many periods of sitting meditation as possible were squeezed into the daily schedule. Apart from meals, the program basically consisted of sitting meditation. Plum Village offered a much greater variety: walking meditation outside in nature, a generous siesta time in the afternoon, and hours of working meditation to keep the center clean and beautiful were sprinkled throughout each day.

I particularly remember enjoying the clock chimes in the dining hall, which sounded every fifteen minutes. With so many people talking at the same time, the room could get quite loud. But when the clock chimed, it suddenly became quiet as everyone followed the practice of bringing their awareness to their breathing and their body for three breaths. This brief peace and quiet transformed the nature of conversation and refreshed the quality with which each person listened and spoke.

I went home after one week, hoping to stay longer in Plum Village someday. One thing led to another, and I spent the next year studying Chinese medicine, almost starting a PhD, and working for a logistics company while I prepared, I hoped, to start my own Chinese medicine practice. Though my whole family celebrated Christmas together and I always very much liked to be there, I decided to return to Plum Village in my free time the next winter. Again, I felt deeply at home. The experience resonated so much that, not long after, I arranged to quit my job and take a short break from my studies to visit Plum Village for ten weeks the following April. Afterward, I thought, I'd take my acupuncture exam and get a degree in teaching mathematics so I could slowly, over time, move in the direction of working as an acupuncturist.

I saw the ten weeks in Plum Village as an important investment in the rest of my life. Being twenty-seven, single, and without a job, I knew it was now or never, and the experience changed my life. Those weeks of mindfulness and practice in community nourished my peace and happiness to an extent I hadn't even begun to imagine. After a few weeks, I realized I wanted to become a monk. All other things—math, Chinese medicine—suddenly seemed unimportant. Being at peace and transmitting this peace to others felt much more meaningful. Day by day, my clarity grew that this was what I really wanted. I knew my parents wouldn't be happy with the prospect of my becoming a monk, though, and I did feel regret when I thought of leaving family and friends.

After living in Plum Village for about five weeks, I decided to share my thoughts with my mother. It was Mother's Day—perhaps not the best day to spring this news on her, but

I had chosen the day carefully. I knew for sure, on this day, she wouldn't be alone. She'd have the support of the whole family. However, when I told her, the festive atmosphere abruptly came to an end. I hoped my family would be more accepting by the time I returned home to take care of my apartment and prepare to return to Plum Village to become a monk, but this was far from reality. Instead, they hoped to change my mind, and my time in the Netherlands became challenging for everybody.

Though my parents and siblings didn't easily accept my choice to ordain, deep down inside I knew I'd always regret it if I didn't become a monk. I yearned for the time and space to transform my suffering and live with intention in community so I could help not only myself, but everyone I encountered.

I met friends to say goodbye and took care of the details, small and large, of leaving. My friend Auke came with a bottle of wine. Since I'd received The Five Mindfulness Trainings in Plum Village, I had committed not to drink alcohol (one of the trainings addresses not consuming substances to suppress your feelings). Yet I couldn't refuse one last farewell drink with a friend. Those were my last drops of alcohol.

After six weeks in the Netherlands, I drove back to Plum Village with my parents, who had agreed to stay with me for a few days. When they asked me "Are you sure?" or "Why did you decide to become a monk for the rest of your life?" I found it difficult to answer. I had no doubts, but the language of my heart couldn't be easily expressed in words. To get around this problem, I said: "I don't know about the far future, but I know in this moment in my life that this is the right decision." On the way back home, my mother lit a candle in a church for me.

Earlier in my life, I could never have imagined becoming a monk, but I have learned that our path is beyond our ability to predict and control. We must let go and flow as a river.

On Taking Action

Breathing involves taking in oxygen. All our cells are dependent on oxygen; without it, we wouldn't survive. We're not the only living beings exchanging air. Outside our body, plants and trees are essential for maintaining healthy air, for example by balancing oxygen and carbon dioxide. Thanks to the trees and other plants, we can survive and enjoy the wonderful miracle of fresh air.

This dependence is abundantly clear when we spend weeks walking through forests, surrounded by trees, plants, and other life. However, it can take more effort to stay connected to the trees and the earth around us in our daily lives at home. Spending truly mindful time outside regularly, even if it's just in a nearby park or right outside of our building, can nourish well-being. Often, it's in these developed environments that we become acutely aware of all the ways humankind has impacted the earth. This awareness, too, is a part of our path to understanding and healing.

When we become aware of how our breathing depends on and contributes to all other living beings, we practice being there for Mother Earth. *Homo sapiens* has spent thousands of years leaving a mark on the ecosystems of the planet. In the last few hundred years, we have emitted so much carbon dioxide and other greenhouse gases into the atmosphere that future generations of all living beings are jeopardized. The roots of environmental pollution are in our mind, engendered by our fears, hatred, greed, and delusions. These emotions and false perceptions are the basis for our actions that lead to pollution.

In Zen, we look at our actions and we also look behind them: we consider how thoughts and speech can also be polluting. Thay offered a series of beautiful phrases (mantras) to say to a loved one to express our love and give them our true presence.

Adapted to address Mother Earth, spending time with these phrases can deepen our connection to the ecosystems around us and support our ability to walk our path with clear eyes and an open heart. We often offer these phrases on mindful hiking retreats and invite you to incorporate them into your own life or time outside in a way that supports you.

The first mantra is *darling, I am here for you*. These words remind us that the gift of our presence is precious. To be truly present for the earth, we can speak this phrase clearly with all our heart. When we speak in this way to Mother Earth, we no longer take her for granted. We are born from her and made of her. Our flesh and bones aren't separate from Mother Earth. When we declare we're here for her, we also declare that we're truly here for ourselves. If we're here for Mother Earth in our own flesh and blood, we'll know how to bear witness as she is strip-mined, as her oceans heat up, as her diverse species go extinct. We cultivate our capacity to offer an unswerving, radical presence.

The second mantra is *I know you are there, and I am happy*. Do we recognize and treasure the presence of Mother Earth from moment to moment? When we do, we feel immediately happy. We stop feeding our anger, fear, and sadness and become aware of all the wholesome conditions and qualities that contribute to our well-being. We recognize and are nourished by the beautiful green mantle of the earth in which we live and thrive—snow-capped mountains, lush green jungles and forests, veins of rivers that sustain life of all sorts.

When we live in forgetfulness, we miss this opportunity. It's not surprising that we engage in thoughts, speech, and actions that poison ourselves and Mother Earth. With the insight that we're a part of the earth and the earth is a part of us—we're one expansive, living organism—we no longer act blindly or recklessly. We don't need to search for happiness by extracting and consuming more resources from the earth and its living species for our own short-lived pleasure and continued dominance. Mindfulness, being truly present, brings happiness now, not at some future time or place.

The third mantra is *I know you suffer, and I want you to know I am here for you*. We don't need to look far or very deeply to see the pain of the animals, plants, and minerals that make up Mother Earth. The signs are all around us. The cells of Gaia suffer—not only human beings, but all the other elements and creatures of the earth. Until we learn to let go of our obsessive grasping at the body of Mother Earth, treating her as a set of resources there merely for our consumption, we'll continue to experience pain, anxiety, fear, and despair due to mass climate migrations, rising sea levels, and the destruction of biodiversity.

Looking with the eyes of interbeing, we see the catastrophic consequences of our actions and let go of our grasping. We see the wonders of life within us and around us, just as they are. Mother Earth provides all the conditions we need to be happy. For this happiness and well-being to endure for thousands of generations into the future, we need to find a collective path of action to bring stability to her climate and balance to her ecosystems.

The fourth mantra is *I suffer; please help*. When we are in pain, it's not easy to ask for help. Because of our pride, we human beings maintain an arrogant and unsustainable attitude toward the earth and other living species. Could it be that the political, economic, and ecological instability we experience today is connected to our own inability to look deeply at the unhealed wounds—both physical and psychological—we inflict on ourselves and others?

The practice of Touching the Earth, bowing down on the earth, can help us to acknowledge and release our own wounds—both personal and collective. Joining our palms, we kneel on the ground and touch our forehead, arms, and legs to the earth in front of us. We let go of all our thoughts and breathe, allowing our pain to flow into the earth. Taking three breaths like this can already help us to let go of our pride and see ourselves as one with Mother Earth. When we take refuge in Mother Earth and touch the Earth in this way, with the awareness that we're not separate entities, we bring about healing. This is how we can ask for help from Mother Earth.

Dear Mother Earth, I am here for you. I know you are there, and I am happy. I know you suffer, and I want you to know I am here for you. I suffer; please help.

MEDITATION
Insight Leads to Action

The following meditation can help us know the habits and tendencies that support wholeness and skillful living as we walk this path together.

> *Breathing in, I am aware of my in-breath. Breathing out, I am aware of my out-breath.*
>
> *In / Out.*
>
> *Breathing in, I am aware the oxygen I inhale fuels combustion in every cell in my body. This oxygen comes from trees and other plants. Breathing out, I am aware I expel carbon dioxide. Some of this carbon dioxide supports the plants around me.*
>
> *From trees / To trees.*

Breathing in, I am aware of the sources of my food. I see the farmer, the truck driver, the soil, the sun, the rain, and the minerals. Looking deeply, I see that plants like nuts, seeds, and legumes need less resources than a hamburger. Breathing out, I smile to the sources of my food.

Sources of food / Smile to sources.

Breathing in, I am aware of the happiness and suffering that make up the food I eat. Breathing out, I feel compassion for the species that may have been harmed to produce my food.

The food I eat / Compassion for harm.

Breathing in, I see the joy of living a simple life. When I know joy right here and now, I know I already have more than enough to be happy. Breathing out, I let go of the idea that happiness lies in the future.

Joy of life / Letting go of future happiness.

Breathing in, I am aware this body is compostable. Breathing out, I take refuge in the earth that I am.

Compostable / Refuge in earth.

Breathing in, I know the joy of connecting and acting with others. Breathing out, I experience the joy of shared aspiration.

Connecting / Joy of shared aspiration.

Bringing It Home

When the insight of interbeing is integrated into our daily life, every action takes on a new quality. We no longer see ourselves as a separate individual, acting in ways that serve only our sphere of interest. Our actions become expansive, capable of bringing benefit—or harm—to the interconnected fabric of living beings. Aware of this, we learn to take better care of our mind in every moment with actions and words that increase kindness, understanding, and joy. As a concrete practice, you may commit to bringing joy to one person in the morning and relieving the suffering of another person in the afternoon. This can be through simple acts like saying a kind word, giving someone a gift, or even just washing the dishes without being asked. Notice what happens as you integrate the path of insightful action rooted in interbeing into your daily life.

CHAPTER TEN

Aimlessness: Medicine for Our Times

Aimlessness Is the Path

PHAP LUU

When I turned twenty-five, after a few years living in Spain and France, I found myself back in my old college town of Hanover, New Hampshire, sleeping on friends' couches until I got a job teaching cross-country skiing and was able to rent a room. Everywhere I looked, a winter wonderland glittered: many days I could clip on my skis right at my back door, ski down onto the ice covering the Connecticut River, cross it, and ski up the hill toward Dartmouth's library, where I liked to spend time reading and studying Zen.

When my lease ran out in March, I decided to sleep outdoors instead of renting a new room. A few undergraduates I'd met at Dartmouth who practiced meditation worked at the organic farm nearby, and for a few weeks I cooked meals with them and slept across the road. I pitched my tent up on a snowdrift each night and nestled into my thirty-degrees-below-zero down sleeping bag. Later I set up closer to campus, locking my bike at the northern entrance to the Appalachian Trail and walking up through the snow to the Velvet Rocks shelter about a mile away. Its entrance was still mostly blocked by snow, but an early hiker had carved a tunnel in, and I slept there cozy as a bear in a cave.

In the mornings I went straight into forty minutes of sitting meditation after waking, focusing on reciting a guided meditation proposed by the Buddha that establishes mindfulness of the body, the feelings, the mind, and all phenomena. This meditation kept me grounded in the present moment and reduced my reactivity and anger. Whenever I felt unable to touch hope, this meditation on establishing mindfulness held me. After having struggled to find a meaningful way to respond to the climate crisis and violence in the world at a global level and suffering from my own unhealed pain due to my parents' divorce as well as some broken personal relationships, this winter was a fresh breath of joy and stability.

The snow melted by late April. I'd found a natural rock shelter hidden in the forest of Velvet Rocks, and each morning I stashed my sleeping bag in a hollow between some rocks. With a brown tarp and some fallen branches, I could create just enough shelter under a rock overhang to be able to lie down out of the rain. I would wake each morning and walk a few hundred feet up to the ridge to sit in meditation as the light started to penetrate the canopy. One morning, a squirrel came and sat on my lap as I meditated, eventually climbing onto my shoulders. While I practiced remaining totally still, accepting whatever pain or pleasure came my way, hermit thrushes saturated the forest near and far with their flutelike overtones—an ancient symphony.

It was after one such morning that four monks walked into the bookstore where I'd begun a part-time job. Corlan Johnson, my boss and the owner of Left Bank Books, usually arrived in the afternoon, so I was alone. I'd been immersed in English translations of early Buddhist texts from the Pali Canon, reading about the lives of forest monks while I sat at the store's front desk. I looked up as the bell on the door tinkled and here, suddenly, were…monks!

As they browsed, I must have blurted out something about meditation. One of the monks offered me an invitation: "Come up to our Day of Mindfulness in South Woodstock. Our center is called Maple Forest Monastery." I felt a strong sense of peace and joy in each of the men now standing in front of me—one young, white, American guy and three older Vietnamese men. Each smiled at me in a gentle, natural way. "Where do I sign up?" I thought.

I cleared my work schedule, rode my bike out to the monastery a few days later, and spent the night sleeping in my tent. The next day, I arrived in the meditation hall to find the monastics listening to a recorded talk in a language I guessed to be Vietnamese while an older nun with a British accent translated. The quality of her voice and the content of her words felt like pure peace speaking right to the deepest recesses within me. As I listened to Thay for the first time and let his reflections on cultivating community sink in, I felt so happy!

When I returned a few weeks later, one of the American nuns invited me and another man to consider staying for the summer family retreat. There were as many lay people, including families and children, as there were monastics, and for the week of the retreat I felt real community around me. The monks and nuns came together for activities—sitting meditation, walking meditation, and Dharma talks—yet they each had their own personalities.

There were elders like Sister Chan Duc and Thay Phap Dang, clearly helping to lead the community; a number of young American monks who giggled and teased each other while making public announcements in the meditation hall; young Vietnamese nuns raised in the West who enjoyed the solitude of nature and sat looking out at the vast expanse of the White Mountains between activities; and nuns and monks who played soccer, slide tackles and all. When Sister Chan Duc gave a Dharma talk on Zen and the Four Establishments of Mindfulness—the essential early teaching I had been meditating with all winter—I felt deeply touched. The combination of Zen and mindfulness that had brought joy back to my life was exactly the central teaching here, in a community that seemed to share my deepest aspirations, a community I could live and grow with.

After the retreat, I hiked into the forest to digest what I'd experienced. The time had felt precious, and I wanted to honor it by offering space, losing myself in wild places with whatever was at work inside of me rather than going straight back into my habitual life. I packed an umbrella-style mosquito net that I could hang from a tree to sit in bug-free meditation and walked south off the monastery grounds.

That first night I slept under the mosquito net out near a swamp and began sitting in meditation when I woke. I'd been studying native edible plants and experimenting with eating what I found, so I waded into the swamp, pulled up a cattail, and cleaned and chewed the root. It would keep me alive if I was starving, I decided, but it wasn't for the faint of heart. Emerging from the forest, I cautiously approached a house from behind and headed down the driveway toward the road. Halfway there, a truck overtook me and a man asked what I was doing. I explained about the monastery and the retreat, and it turned out the man's wife was a Thai Buddhist and that he himself had heard about Maple Forest Monastery. With spontaneous generosity, he invited me in for breakfast with his family and soon I was enjoying pancakes and eggs—a step up from mealy cattail roots.

This was the first of many lessons I would learn on my path of aimlessness, of living, breathing, and hiking Zen: often when we think we can manage everything on our own, living off roots and fruits while cut off from society, we forget the friendliness of our fellow human beings. Although hurt feelings I hadn't taken care of in the past lingered and sometimes made me consider leaving human society entirely when I was young, time and again I found myself pulled back by the inherent kindness of strangers.

After breakfast, I continued wandering south. By evening I found myself at the foot of a mountain rising majestically over the Connecticut River. That night, the wind picked up and there were strange, scraping noises outside my tent. Faced with the unknown, the mind has many ideas: Was it a bear? A wolf? A murderous ghost or a human? Or just branches creaking in the night?

The next morning, I approached a flank of the mountain and came upon a wondrous flock of turkeys in a clearing. It felt like coming on an ancient gathering of dinosaurs moving through the Cretaceous jungle. I stopped and watched them as they jutted their heads and poked in the grass for seeds, worms, and insects. Kicking off my sandals, I continued barefoot on the soft earth, aware of my breath and of everything unfolding within and around me as I moved up through the pines adorning the mountainside.

I reached the summit after hours of gentle steps in the rich humus of mountain soil and looked out onto the vast green expanse of Vermont. *It is enough to die right now,* I thought, *breathing in such beauty!* Since then, I've had this thought thousands of times: *living each moment fully is already enough.* Why are we so obsessed with our projects; why do we let our worry eat away at the joy of living? With the immense spirit of the mountain in my heart, I descended toward the Connecticut River below.

After a quick stop in a country store for a much-relished sandwich and re-supply, I headed out on railroad tracks that paralleled the river. A few hours on, I spotted a washed-out drain opening onto a stony beach with piles of driftwood and flotsam. Having grown up on a lake formed by a dammed river, I was used to the sort of stuff that washes up onshore—whitened branches, bark stripped by water and sunlight, tires, Styrofoam, bottles, plastic cords. Random bits of civilization.

Thinking of the Buddha's teaching that the practice and the community surrounding it is a raft upon which you cross to the other shore (and remembering one of my favorite books, *Huckleberry Finn*), I set to building a raft. After lashing driftwood together and securing floats and bottles underneath, in five or six hours I stood under the blazing midday sun, admiring the semblance of a raft I'd created. I heaved my backpack onto the platform to keep it away from splashing water, crawled aboard, and pushed off into the river.

The day passed as I sat in meditation on the raft, an otter occasionally circling me. The banks of the river slid by; a gentle current carried me southward. Occasionally, I used a long pole to direct the raft away from the shore. With no rudder, the raft circled lazily in the eddies along the way, lulling me to sleep as I lay down on my side. Evening arrived. I enjoyed a deep, restful sleep after the agitation of the noises the night before.

I woke in the morning to find the raft nestled against the river's eastern shore, at rest in the shallows. I had crossed to the other shore! Smiling at the joyful outcome of my aimlessness, I sat with this moment, with this breath, before crossing with the pole back to the Vermont side. Without much ceremony, I pushed the raft off, back into the river's flow. Couldn't I, as a monk, live like this, my life packed on my back, walking from place to place in stages, meditating in wild places, sleeping on the earth, breathing forest air, and relying for sustenance on the generosity of strangers?

This vision came from what I'd learned about the life of the historical Buddha, who realized being dependent every day on the generosity of others was the most immediate way for monks and nuns to practice humility. Living with no money in this way required the cultivation of moment-by-moment unconditional love and trust; it meant deeply embracing aimlessness, something that now feels so countercultural even the word *aimless* has negative connotations. I watched my raft circle lazily downstream and then lifted my pack and continued on my way.

Having now walked the path of aimlessness for the decades between that day and this one, I'm not afraid not to know what's coming. I'm freed by not having to pretend that I could know.

On Aimlessness

As Zen monks, aimlessness is at the heart of our lives: no moment is a means to an end—ends and means are one. On our mindful hiking retreats, we do bring a map. We have an idea of where we're going to sleep each night. And yet, we practice letting go of our expectations in every moment. We call this the practice of aimlessness. In every Zen tradition, aimlessness is a door of liberation—walking through this door is a way of moving toward freedom and awakening. Aimlessness is an antidote to the anxiety caused by our conviction that we are in control of our life and ought to be constantly making sure things go our way, implementing a detailed plan that will bring us unfailingly to the outcomes we desire.

Touching aimlessness in our lives can be frightening. We crave certainty in our career, our relationships, and our spiritual direction. We see immense suffering and injustice in the world, and we deeply desire to alleviate it. Yet if we wish to wake up to our deepest nature, to a place from which we can act with wisdom and capacity in complex and overwhelming conditions, we need to be able to let go of all expectations. Our expectations may be the biggest obstacle to our happiness, to our ability to stay grounded and engaged in heartfelt ways.

Though it can be overwhelming, awareness of our mortality has been central to Zen wisdom since its earliest days. Understanding that the moments given to us in this life are not infinite leads us to be fully present in each one of them. If you explore this kind of practice, you may find that, rather than being morbid or depressing, awareness of your limited time can create gratitude and a new freshness in each moment. Living this way, we're freed from the tension of scrambling to maintain the delusion that we are ultimately in control. We can let go of the expectation that we will arrive somewhere in the future. We can open to aimlessness, focusing on each moment.

In meditation, we notice whether our mind is fixed on or obsessed with a goal of any sort, and then we let go of it. We focus on cultivating complete presence in every moment, trusting that the path will manifest in front of us with each breath and each step. Applied to hiking, aimlessness means arriving with each step, flexible and adaptable no matter what comes next. If our mind is occupied with worries or plans, we can leave them behind by directing all our attention to the contact of our feet with the earth. We can practice arriving in the present moment with each step we take. When we walk on soft soil, we can often see our own footprints. We leave other traces as well. With each mindful step, we imprint not only the weight of our body, but also our peace, joy, and freedom on Mother Earth. When practicing aimlessness, we have a path to walk on, we have a direction, but no thought of a destination. The present moment, walking on the path, is our destination.

Making space for aimlessness in a hiking retreat can be challenging. One hiker in a retreat in Nepal comes to mind. He worried repeatedly about the potential for bad weather each afternoon and wanted to arrive as soon as possible at each tea house where we had arranged to sleep. Though our walk was quite safe—we had a trusted guide, a well-worn path, and many local people in the towns nearby ready to provide us food and shelter—worry drove him on. He had difficulty experiencing peace in the present moment.

With the support of the whole community over ten days of mindful hiking, his worry decreased, and the moments when he could enjoy the camaraderie of the group at whatever pace we were going increased. Even when it rained, he could enjoy walking in the rain. In our sharing groups during the retreat, he spent less and less time obsessing about when we would arrive at our destination and began to enjoy every moment more deeply. He saw and felt that we were not worried, that aimlessness could relieve his own worry, and began to take in more of the beauty of the vast mountains and forests. He got a taste of Zen.

A Compassionate and Nonviolent Future

PHAP LUU

On the final day of our seven-week Appalachian Trail trek, our two hiking groups meet in the last campsite west of Georgetown to walk together into Washington, DC. Throughout our hike, we have arrived, we are home in each step. We acted from peace and freedom rather than fear and selfishness. More than fifty people walking in silence, we enter Georgetown, where local sangha members begin to appear left and right, joining our silent walk for its final mile.

Leaving the forest yet carrying it with us, within us, the climate catastrophe is in all our hearts and minds. Those of us with a broad view of history wonder what role the American Empire will play in the ongoing destabilization of ecological systems and the consequent refugee crises; we wonder what role we will play. Not knowing, we continue to put one foot in front of the other as we've done since leaving the Great Togetherness meditation hall of Blue Cliff Monastery, walking as we've done our entire lives.

The concrete under our feet is hard. We no longer tread atop pine needles, composting leaves, and melting snow. Yet, even here, we breathe with the trees. Our steps lead us ever closer to the spot where Thay sat after walking with staff from the World Bank to the National Mall. We approach the reflection pool where Dr. Martin Luther King Jr. stood on August 28, 1963, when he spoke the words that would be inscribed thereafter in the heart of every American child. "We cannot walk alone," Dr. King said, in his historic "I Have a Dream" speech.

Martin Luther King Jr.'s dream of building a "Beloved Community" is what Thay vowed to continue when he heard Dr. King had been killed. On April 5, 1968, the day after the assassination, Thay wrote:

> I did not sleep last night. I am afraid the root of violence is so deep in the heart and mind and manner of this society. This country is able to produce King but

cannot preserve King. I am sorry for you. For me.
For all of us.

Standing in silence, we look down upon the pool and come back to our breathing. Together, we realize the dream of Beloved Community here and now. Our mindfulness practice, like Thay's, can't be separated from anything we do. As our awareness gathers and our hearts open, we will inevitably engage with the challenges and pain that surround us. None of us can be free alone.

Above us, the modern Washington Monument pierces a blue sky, and its starkness makes the one we discovered in Maryland days before seem archaic and humble. How much longer will this empire exert its dominance—symbolized by this piercing obelisk? What will future generations, if they exist at all, learn from the ruins of our civilization, from the Anthropocene? Will future species walk among the ruins of the US Capitol as we now do in the Roman Forum, wondering at the decayed structures, trying to imagine what life in their shadow was like? What will become of a country that has concentrated military power with a wealth unmatched by any other?

These questions don't feel theoretical as we come back to our breathing. In the spirit of aimlessness, not knowing at the outset whether we would walk this far, we arrive, a half-dozen brown-robed Zen monks and many more community members, at the secular locus of world power. Future generations depend on the story we write with our every step, our every breath, our every action. Aware of this, we continue walking and turn left, flowing as one body to the Vietnam Veterans Memorial.

Sky, father-in-law to Joydeep and grandfather to Joydeep's twelve-year-old son Aidan, joined the hike the previous week along with his family. He'd been in the Marines in Vietnam. For him, walking mindfully in accordance with the teachings of a Vietnamese Zen Master who himself suffered and faced exile as a result of the same war created a uniquely powerful moment. He and the rest of us do our best to be mindful of our steps as our eyes keep going back to the lists of casualties: name after name carved in stone.

I ask myself: *Will there be future monuments to the casualties of our reckless war with the earth?*

Past the memorial, we arrive in a grassy clearing and discover more of the sangha. More than a hundred people have come to greet us and walk in mindfulness. Now close to two hundred strong, we circle Constitution Gardens Pond, walking in peace, walking in freedom. When we come to where Thay sat in 2013, we, too, sit. We face toward the White House, fold our legs, and come back to our breathing—no violence, no aggression. Together we hold the suffering of generations. Our hearts are full of questions. I hold up a small bell and silently recite a gatha before letting it sound:

Body, speech, and mind in perfect oneness
I send my heart along with the sound of the bell
May those who hear it awaken from forgetfulness
And transcend the path of anxiety and sorrow.

The sound of the bell rings out clearly onto the Mall, into the trees, and down to the water of the pond. A compassionate and nonviolent future is possible, if we know how to make peace with the earth. Together, we sit, our minds trained by the woods and our aimless hike to coalesce in peace and freedom, for the benefit of all beings.

Walking Between Trees

How would you walk if you knew you were taking the last steps of your life, if you knew nothing more would happen for you—no work, no events, no concerns, no joys—after you arrived at your destination? Imagine walking between two trees, one your birth and the other your death. If you knew the second tree was the end, wouldn't you enjoy every step along the way completely, savoring each one? Wouldn't you stop rushing to get to your so-called "destination?" Even taking a handful of steps between two trees in a small stretch of forest, two clumps of grass in a field, or two fence posts in your backyard, you can come alive to the wonder of nature, your body, and the gift of life.

Mary Oliver asks, "What is it you plan to do with your one wild and precious life?"[9] Our young imaginations fill with possibilities. Yet, as our life progresses, we see our time here is incredibly short. What *will* we do with it? Walking between two trees, or from any one point to another, as if they spanned the length of our life helps us train our mind to recognize this present moment is already enough; if we die tomorrow, our life—our wishes, our dreams, our goals—is already accomplished. It's enough to live fully in this present moment, just taking a step. When we take care of our body and mind in this way, we realize what is most human, what is most real, what is most meaningful about living on this planet Earth. Nothing more needs to be done. The next step will follow.

Walking between two trees is a rich practice Thay offered to us. We encourage you to practice out in nature in a quiet place. Leave behind any mobile phone or gadgets. Go analog. You have enough distractions in your own mind; when cultivating peace and calm, do not add distractions from outside.

Find a place outside in nature without too many disturbances or distractions.

Find two trees to serve as the two points between which you will walk. If you aren't in a forested area, you can use other plants, stones, logs, or anything else easily identifiable.

Come back to your breathing and start your walking meditation at the first tree or point, seeing the second tree as truly the end point—even the end of your life.

Notice as you walk: Can you sink into this practice of letting go of everything—all your projects, all your concerns, all your ideas—and fully enjoy your breath with each step? Can you walk just to walk, knowing one day your steps will end?

You may notice your steps becoming slower as you come closer to the second tree. Be gentle with yourself. Use mindfulness to embrace any emotion that comes up—fear, anxiety, worry. Train yourself to embrace the unknown.

See if you can set aside a few minutes each day for this practice for a week or longer. It may elicit strong emotions in you, and it's important to give your heart and mind the chance to settle.

Bringing It Home

You can adapt this practice to work in your backyard or even take it into your built landscape by using two pieces of furniture, walls, or the beginning and end of a stairway. Practice walking between these with full presence, as if these are the last steps you will take. Wherever we are, we can choose a path of happiness, which is a path of presence. Wherever we are, the path is our sacred path: a path where we are mindful, peaceful, and free. Breathing in, we can touch the nature of aimlessness and, at least for a moment, let go of any goal.

What insights arise after a few days of this practice? How do you feel different in body and mind? Do you really feel peaceful and free? Do you have conditions to be happy in the present moment, even if you need to look again? Consider expressing your experience through journaling, drawing, painting, or sharing your insights and experiences with a friend.

AFTERWORD

Where to Go from Here?

Thank you for coming on this journey with us. This book is open-ended, waiting for you to write the next chapter with your own experiences of mindful walking in nature. Though we are monks, we do not see ourselves primarily as teachers, but rather as seekers, fellow friends on the path. As we witness the ever-increasing preoccupation with material things that characterizes our age, we need more stories from people like you, people choosing another way: the path of freedom, the path of happiness.

We are deeply concerned about our planet. The climate crisis and our political polarization increasingly threaten our collective well-being. Yet these disasters closely parallel the lowering of borders, the weakening of nationalism, and the growing consciousness that we are one family of living beings on Planet Earth and must treat it and ourselves accordingly. *Hiking Zen* is a small contribution to the collective transformation of consciousness already very much underway.

What is your deepest aspiration? This is not something anyone can tell you. It comes from your own insight. The practices in this book can build a foundation for realizing this kind of insight. Our experiences walking in nature brought us the space and introspection necessary to find our own insights, which we now apply in our daily lives and share here with you.

Where to go from here? Let your heart be your guide. For some of us, just a few minutes walking in a park every day with mindfulness will be enough — and the most we can do. Others may need a radical shift, as the two of us did — to embark on a longer trek, to live in a different way, or even to become monastics committed in every moment to the path of awakening. Some may feel even this step is not enough — like the Buddha, some may need to forge their own path, outside of any existing form.

Wherever your steps take you, may this book — the offering of two Zen monks transformed by wild places and the community surrounding us — always serve as a refuge when the going gets rough. Take whatever step calls to you, however radical or seemingly mundane. We've got your back. You can leave behind business as usual; you can bring openhearted mindfulness to whatever life you live; you can take the path that returns you to your deepest and most intimate humanity. Know that we're with you, every step of the way.

From Thay, through us, to you, a benediction for your winding trail:

Our True Heritage

The cosmos is filled with precious gems.
I want to offer a handful of them to you this morning.
Each moment you are alive is a gem,
shining through and containing earth and sky,
water and clouds.
You only need to breathe lightly
for the miracles to be displayed.

Suddenly you hear the birds singing,
the pines chanting;
you see the flowers blooming,
the blue sky,
the white clouds,
the smile and the marvelous look
of your beloved.
You, the richest person on Earth,
who has been going around begging for a living,
stop being the destitute child.
Come back and claim your true heritage.
We should enjoy our happiness
and offer it to everyone.
Cherish this very moment.
Let go of the river of suffering
and embrace life fully in your arms.[10]

Bon voyage and happy trails!

Brother Phap Luu (right) and Brother Phap Man walking out of Wurtsboro on an old railroad track, part of the Shawangunk Trail headed south to its juncture with the Appalachian Trail at High Point, New Jersey, during the first week of the seven-week journey. (Photo credit: Ramon Carreras)

Recipes for Mindful Walking in Community

You can put the exercises in this book into practice immediately on your own, even if you have only a few square meters in which to walk. One of Thay's students, a political prisoner during the war in Vietnam, had only a small cell in which to diligently practice mindful walking throughout the day, so that was what she did to keep her mind calm and clear. In comparison, most of us have far more spacious conditions—look at the conditions you have right here and now!

Once you've experienced the power of mindful walking in nature on your own, we encourage you to share the practice with others. It may be easier at first to practice walking meditation with others already familiar with the practice. If you're not already connected with a sangha (a community of mindfulness practitioners), take a look at the Plum Village sangha directory, which is available online. Consider joining a sangha and suggesting one of the "recipes" below as a sangha activity. Once you're solid in your own practice of mindful walking in nature, you may like to introduce it to friends unfamiliar with this sort of thing. This can be a wonderful gift to offer, even if (or perhaps because) they are unused to walking in company in silence, to coming back to their breath, or to being truly present with their slow and gentle steps on the earth.

If you intend to lead a backpacking retreat with a group of friends or participants, please seriously consider undergoing

Wilderness First Aid or Wilderness First Responder training (or the equivalent in your country) or hiring a guide who has this training. Even if you have previous backpacking experience, it helps to review the wealth of excellent material available—such as *Backpacker Magazine*'s "The Complete Guide to Backpacking"—so you can respond effectively to whatever situations arise on the trail. Many organizations train potential hike leaders in expedition planning; the National Outdoor Leadership School (NOLS) or Outward Bound are great places to look. Of course, you can also go on a mindful hiking retreat organized by a Plum Village practice center, such as Deer Park Monastery or the European Institute of Applied Buddhism, or with an organization doing similar work (such as Inward Bound Mindfulness if you're a teenager or young adult).

The recipes below range from simple one-hour events to more complex, multi-day journeys. Each has been thoroughly tested on our Hiking Zen retreats, but please use your discretion to adapt them to your own situation.

1. Mindful Walk in Nature
(30 MINS TO 1.5 HOURS)

Gather the group in a circle. In the Plum Village tradition, we prepare for a mindful walk while singing Plum Village songs like "Breathing In, Breathing Out," "I Have Arrived, I Am Home," or "The Mind Can Go in a Thousand Directions," all of which are conveniently available in the Plum Village app if you wish to learn them. After a few songs, you'll probably notice everyone is a bit more relaxed and open.

When you feel ready, begin to speak about the practice of walking meditation: encourage everyone to coordinate their breathing with their steps, to bring awareness to the contact of the soles of their feet with the earth, to let go of thinking about the future or the past, and to smile. It's a joy and a privilege to walk on the earth! If you embody this joy, it will inspire those around you to go deeper into the practice of mindful walking. On our Plum Village-style hiking retreats, we frequently share texts from the book *Touching the Earth*.[11] Although the texts are conceived as intimate conversations with the Buddha, you can come up with your own versions of intimate conversations with whatever or whomever is sacred and dear to you. You may like to say, "Dear Earth," for example. If you feel inspired to share a *Touching the Earth* passage aloud, "Mindful Walking" works well:

Mindful Walking

Dear Buddha [or alternative], I feel warm in my heart every time I am able to talk to and confide in you. I feel your presence in every cell of my body and know you are listening with compassion to everything I say. You walked on this planet Earth as a free person. I also want to walk on Planet Earth as a free person.

Around me are people who do not walk as free people. They only know how to run. They run into the future because they think that happiness cannot be found in the present moment. They are walking on the earth but their minds are up in the clouds. They walk like sleepwalkers, without knowing where they are going. I know I also have the habit to lose my peace and freedom as I walk.

Dear Buddha, I vow to follow your example and always walk as someone who is free and awake. I vow that in every step I take my feet will truly touch the earth and I shall be aware that I am walking on the ground of reality and not in a dream. Walking like that, I am in touch with everything that is wonderful and miraculous in the universe. I vow to walk in such a way that my feet will be able to impress on the earth the seal of freedom and peace. I know that steps taken like this have the capacity to heal my body and mind as well as Planet Earth itself.

While I practice walking meditation outside with the sangha, I vow to be aware that it is a great happiness to walk with the sangha. With each step, I am aware that I am not a solitary drop of water but am part of a river. With mindful breathing and steps, I shall produce the energy of mindfulness and concentration that contributes to the collective mindfulness of the sangha. I shall open my body and mind so that the collective energy of our sangha can enter me, protect me, and help me to gently flow along like a river, harmonizing myself with everything that is. I know that by entrusting my body and mind, as well as my painful feelings, to the sangha that they may be embraced and healed. In this way I shall be nourished as I am practicing mindful walking with the sangha and make significant transformation in my body and mind. In the meditation hall I shall open myself to the sangha's energy as I practice slow walking meditation, taking one step for my in-breath and one step for my out-breath. I vow to walk in such a way that every step can nourish myself and my sangha with the energy of freedom and solidity.

Remind everyone to stay together while walking to create a supportive energy for the group. Whoever leads the walk must extend their awareness not only to their own breath and steps but also to the breath and steps of others walking with them, noticing anyone's tendency to rush, fall behind, or stomp heavily on the earth, for example. The leader's mindfulness practice has a significant impact on the group.

There are so many ways we walk as a community on the earth: as friends out for a stroll and also as refugees escaping a volatile political situation, as activists in a peace demonstration, as soldiers in a military operation, as hunters coordinating a hunt. Knowing we're interconnected with all ecosystems and beings, we see elements of all these many ways of walking in ourselves and walk in such a way that we transform the capacity for violence and hatred in our hearts into kindness, compassion, and peace. We imprint what's in our own heart on the earth.

The leader can bring along a small bell. It's nice to stop from time to time and invite one or three sounds of the bell so everyone can enjoy mindfulness while standing silently, breathing, and noticing the beauty around them.

It's helpful to walk in a loop, returning to the starting point so no one loses their orientation or finds themselves unable to return to their bike, car, or residence at the end of the walk. You may like to close the walk by gathering in a circle and inviting everyone to speak briefly about their experience.

2. Mindful Day Hike

(3–9 HOURS)

You may like to spend an entire morning, afternoon, or day walking together with others in nature. A day hike could include one or two meals or snacks prepared in advance as well as plenty of water that participants pack and carry with them. Plan the hike so you won't have to rush to finish on time. It's okay to come back earlier than planned.

Be aware that there are different strengths in each group. As a group you may go slower than most would go as separate individuals. Temper the speed to the inclination of the group and pace yourself based on the slowest person. Walk to cultivate mindfulness—be aware of our tendency to rush or walk quickly and learn to transform these habits into the joy of just being present with our breath and our steps, no matter the pace. Forget any destination.

Start out in a circle as above, with songs and a short inspiring introduction to mindful walking. You may like to add what's called "second body practice," in which each person checks in and looks after another person for the day as their "second body." We all have our first body that we take care of in every moment. What's it like to look after another's body? After breaks, before we start again, we look to see where our second body is and how they're doing. This builds a sense of connection and ensures we don't inadvertently leave anyone behind.

Reading a passage from *Touching the Earth* before setting off can imbue your hiking with mindfulness. You may like to read one, two, or three inspirational passages throughout the day to offer a focus for the group's journey. In addition to the passage on mindful walking shared above, you may like to read "Recognizing Feelings and Emotions" and "Nourishing Our Ancestors and Our Descendants" to inspire your next hike.

Recognizing Feelings and Emotions

Dear Buddha, thanks to practicing mindful breathing and walking, I am aware of what is happening around me. I can recognize the different mental formations as they arise in me. I know that the wounds of my ancestors and my parents, as well as wounds from my childhood until now, still lie deep in my consciousness. Sometimes painful feelings associated with sadness rise up in me and if I do not know how to recognize, embrace, and help them to calm down, I can say things and do things that cause division or a split in my family or my community. When I cause division around me, I also feel divided in myself. Dear Buddha, I am determined to remember your teachings, to practice mindful breathing and walking and produce more positive energy in my daily life. I can use this energy to recognize the painful feelings in me and help them to calm down. I know that suppressing these feelings and emotions when they come up will only make the situation more difficult.

Dear Buddha, thanks to your teachings, I know that these feelings and emotions for the most part arise from narrow perceptions and incomplete understanding. I have wrong ideas about myself and about other people. I have ideas about happiness and about suffering that I cannot let go of and that is what makes me suffer. I have already made myself suffer a great deal because of my ideas. For example, I have the idea that happiness and suffering come from outside of myself and are not due to my own mind. My way of looking, listening, understanding, and judging has made me suffer and has made my loved ones suffer. I know that by letting go of these ideas I will be happier and more peaceful in my body and mind. Letting go of my narrow ideas and wrong perceptions, my painful feelings and emotions will no longer have a basis to arise.

Dear Buddha, I know that I still have so many wrong perceptions that prevent me from seeing things as they really are. I promise that from now on I shall practice looking deeply to see that the majority of my suffering arises from my ideas and perceptions. I shall not blame others when I suffer, but return to myself and recognize the source of my suffering in my misperceptions and my lack of deep understanding. I shall practice looking deeply, letting go of wrong perceptions and helping other people let go of their wrong perceptions so that they can also overcome their suffering.

Nourishing Our Ancestors and Descendants

Dear Buddha, in the Avatamsaka Sutra you have taught that the one contains the all, and that the present contains not only the past but also the future. When I look deeply into the present I can touch the future. I can be in touch with all my descendants because the future generations are already in me in this present moment. I am aware that when I look after myself well in the present I am looking after my descendants. When I have true love and compassion for myself, I have love and compassion for them. Whatever I offer myself, I offer them. One thing I can offer myself many times a day are the mindful steps that I make with solidity, peace, and freedom. Every step like that nourishes me, my ancestors in me, and all the generations of descendants which are present in me waiting to manifest.

Another gift I can offer is every mindful breath, which brings about peace and freedom. This gift brings joy and life to me, my ancestors, and my descendants in this present moment. When I eat, I also nourish the body and the spirit of my ancestors and descendants. When I practice sitting meditation, I nourish my ancestors and descendants spiritually. My deep desire is to devote every moment of my practice to nourishing my ancestors and descendants. I am aware that every step, every breath, every smile, every look made in mindfulness is an act of true love. I do not want to nourish myself with toxic foods, whether they are edible food, the food of sense impression, the food of intention, or the food of consciousness. I vow that I shall not consume any products that are toxic, whether food or drink, books, magazines, films, music or conversations. I do not want to nourish my ancestors and descendants with products that contain the toxins of craving, hatred, violence, and despair. I only want to nourish and offer to my ancestors and descendants wholesome foods that nourish, purify, and transform. I know that the practice of mindful consumption is the most effective way to protect myself, my ancestors, and my descendants. Consuming mindfully, I express my deepest respect and love for myself, for my ancestors, and all my descendants.

The only thing that I wish to transmit to my descendants, within me and outside of me, is the fruits of my daily practice — the energies of understanding and love. The only words and actions that I want to transmit to others are those which come from right view, right thinking, and right speech. I vow to live the present moment in such a way that I can guarantee a bright future for my descendants. I know that if my descendants are alive in me in the present time then I also will be alive in my descendants in the future.

For meals, you may like to eat in silence for ten to twenty minutes after three sounds of the bell and a reading of the Five Contemplations, shared below. If the group is large and your voice isn't audible at a distance, you may like to read the contemplations aloud standing together before everyone spreads out to find a place to sit. Encourage people, through your own example, to eat mindfully and share their food.

Contemplations Before Eating

This food is a gift of the earth, the sky, numerous living beings, and much hard and loving work.

May we eat with mindfulness and gratitude so as to be worthy to receive this food.

May we recognize and transform unwholesome mental formations, especially our greed and learn to eat with moderation.

May we keep our compassion alive by eating in such a way that reduces the suffering of living beings, stops contributing to climate change, and heals and preserves our precious planet.

We accept this food so that we may nurture our brotherhood and sisterhood, build our sangha, and realize our ideal of serving all living beings.

At the end of the session, notice if the group feels refreshed, relaxed, and more present. Notice if people are feeling worn down and exhausted. Consider how you might restructure the day the next time; for example, you may like to add more breaks for water, food, or the bathroom. See each hike as an opportunity to learn.

3. Mindful Hiking or Backpacking Retreat

(3–7 DAYS)

A hiking retreat requires more forethought than a day hike, because you'll need to assess the capacity of participants beforehand. This can be done by calling each of them and asking about previous hiking experience—what distances they have walked, what kind of footwear they used, the quality of the experience. The physical abilities of each participant should be such that significant physical challenges won't define the hiking retreat. A mindful hike isn't a competition, nor should it be difficult. Give everyone a sense of how much distance you plan to cover each day and make sure they feel comfortable with the distances proposed.

Encourage each participant to spend one or two days on a hike near their home carrying a day pack loaded with whatever they plan to bring on the retreat. This will help them to gauge their own capacity. These practice hikes should include elevation gains (hills) comparable to the terrain planned for the retreat. Even after you've communicated the importance of the practice hikes, keep in mind that people tend to overestimate their capacity. Make sure you always have a backup plan for anyone who may want to leave the retreat early. On the trail, we've dealt with such problems as panic leading to asthma attacks, emotional turmoil, the popping of painkillers to push through pain, debilitating blisters, fevers, sore or injured joints, and altitude sickness.

Basecamp-supported mindful hiking—as opposed to mindful backpacking—is logistically the easiest multi-day retreat to organize. Everyone just needs a small day pack, and at the end of each day they come back to the same place to sleep. No one needs to carry much weight each day. With a basecamp, you really don't have to arrive anywhere. You don't have to reach a certain destination each day; you can be a little more flexible. People can come back early from the hike or take a rest day if they don't feel well. The leader(s) can decide between out-and-back and loop walks each day. In places where public transport is accessible, someone can be available to drive a car, or you can hire transportation. There is the possibility of hiking one-way to a meeting point and getting shuttled back to the basecamp or shuttling to a starting point in the morning and spending the day returning home.

Of course, the possibilities of a backpacking retreat where everyone carries their sleeping gear and the group brings enough food for the days they'll be out are special and inspiring in their own way. Such a retreat requires more equipment and more planning. Which type of multi-day retreat you organize depends on you, your group, and the infrastructure you have. Whether you're backpacking or going on a series of day hikes together, start each day's hike with song and inspiration as described in the mindful day hike recipe above.

Notes on the Practice of Touching the Earth

Touching the Earth, mentioned here and there throughout this book, is a practice that restores our sacred connection with the earth. We often use texts from the book *Touching the Earth: 46 Guided Meditations for Mindfulness Practice* when we guide the activities suggested here. You may like to have someone read a passage to the group before heading out on a hike.

If the group is inspired to do so, you may also do the full practice of Touching the Earth, which is not dissimilar to a sun salutation in yoga. Stand listening to the text with palms joined at the heart, and when the person guiding the activity finishes the reading, bring your joined palms up to touch your forehead before spreading your hands and arms out wide as you bend your knees to the ground and place your forehead, arms, and knees on the earth, your palms turned up toward the sky. You are embracing the earth.

You may like to have a mat to rest on, or you may prefer the more visceral experience of bowing down directly onto the dirt or grass. After breathing in and out mindfully and slowly at least three times, the one guiding the practice invites a sound of the bell, and everyone stands up again with palms joined. Touch the earth three times after the reading of each text—for many people, it is a grounding practice to embrace Mother Earth.

We've included a reference to the *Touching the Earth* text in each day of the following two sets of multi-day retreat plans for you to incorporate if you'd like. On a multi-day retreat, you can offer a progression of meditation topics to practice with each day. For a seven-day retreat, for example, we often use the following progression:

Day 1: Arrival Day/Orientation

Day 2: Mindful Breathing ("Walking in Freedom")

Day 3: Mindful Walking ("Mindful Walking")

Day 4: Recognizing Feelings and Emotions ("Recognizing Feelings and Emotions")

Day 5: Nourishing Our Ancestors and Our Descendants ("Nourishing Our Ancestors and Our Descendants")

Day 6: Interbeing ("Oneness with All Beings")

Day 7: How to Bring the Practice Home / Departure

For a ten-day retreat, you may like to explore the following progression:

Day 1: Arrival Day/Orientation

Day 2: Mindful Breathing ("Walking in Freedom")

Day 3: Mindful Walking ("Mindful Walking")

Day 4: Being with Our Senses ("Living in the Present")

Day 5: Recognizing Feelings and Emotions ("Recognizing Feelings and Emotions")

Day 6: Nourishing Our Ancestors and Our Descendants ("Nourishing Our Ancestors and Our Descendants")

Day 7: The River of Life ("The River of Life")

Day 8: Interbeing ("Oneness with All Beings")

Day 9: Riding the Waves of Birth and Death ("Riding the Waves of Birth and Death")

Day 10: How to Bring the Practice Home / Departure

You may like to incorporate *Touching the Earth* texts throughout the day; feel free to find passages that resonate with you or with what the group is experiencing.

NOTES

1　For more gathas, see *Stepping into Freedom: An Introduction to Bud-dhist Monastic Training* by Thich Nhat Hanh, translated by Annabel Laity, second edition, (Parallax Press, 2021).

2　For more on Sister Kaira Jewel's journey, see her book: Kaira Jewel Lingo, *We Were Made for These Times: Ten Lessons on Moving Through Change, Loss, and Disruption* (Parallax Press, 2021).

3　Daniel E. Lieberman, *The Evolution of the Human Head* (The Belknap Press of Harvard University Press, 2011), https://doi.org/10.4159/9780674059443.

4　See M. León-Mejía, M. Gutiérrez-Ortega, I. Serrano-Pintado, J. González-Cabrera, "A systematic review on nomophobia prevalence: Surfacing results and standard guidelines for future research," *PLoS ONE* 16(5): e0250509. https://doi.org/10.1371/journal.pone.0250509.

5　See The Five Mindfulness Trainings at https://plumvillage.org/mindfulness/the-5-mindfulness-trainings.

6　See "Letter to the CEO of Kentucky Fried Chicken," *In Love and Trust: Letters from a Zen Master* by Thich Nhat Hanh and Dinh Nghiem (Parallax Press, 2024) 260–2.

7　See John Long, "Meet the Ancestors," *Australasian Science*, vol. 26, no. 3, Control Publications Pty Ltd, 2005, 18–23, and Neil Shubin, *Your Inner Fish: The Amazing Discovery of Our 375-Million-Year-Old Ancestor* (Penguin, 2009).

8　The details that follow are found in Simon Plugge's narrative, *Recollections*, given to my father by Simon Plugge. It is not yet publicly available. —Brother Phap Xa

9   "The Summer Day," Mary Oliver, *New and Selected Poems* (Boston: Beacon Press, 2005), 94.

10 "Our True Heritage" by Thich Nhat Hanh can be found in *Call Me by My True Names* (Berkeley, CA: Parallax Press, 2022).

11 Thich Nhat Hanh, *Touching the Earth: 46 Guided Meditations for Mindfulness Practice*, revised edition (Parallax Press, 2008).

ACKNOWLEDGMENTS

Writing this book has been a deeply transformative and rewarding experience for both of us. Seven years with many ups and downs have passed since we began, including the passing of our teacher, Zen Master Thich Nhat Hanh, in 2022. Most of what is good in this book comes directly from his teachings; we only dare to write it because of his constant encouragement for both of us to speak from our own experience of putting these teachings into practice. No words can express our gratitude to him.

In the process of reflection and writing this book, Brother Phap Xa has felt deep gratitude toward his family for supporting him on every step of his monastic path, even though his decision to become a monk was hard to accept. Thank you Freek, Riek, Alma, Janwillem, and Judeke Frederiks! Brother Phap Luu thanks his family for their unwavering support: Susan Bachman, Frank Bachman, and Kerry Whiting—and cousin Michelle Buckingham.

We would both like to thank Jon Kabat-Zinn for graciously agreeing to write the foreword to this book—even when he had declared he was done writing forewords. Thank you for fulfilling your karmic assignment. Your friendship and mentorship have been invaluable.

We are grateful to the entire team at Parallax for believing in this book. We are deeply grateful for the skillful guidance, love, and precious time of our excellent editor at Parallax Press, Miranda Perrone, who saw right away the value in what we were doing and has been central to shaping it into the form you have now in your hands. If there is anything in the book that misses its mark, it is because we pushed against her sage advice. Parallax's publisher, Hisae Matsuda, has been a great cheerleader for this book since its conception and has contributed essential edits. Jacob Surpin, now at Penguin Random House, also gave us wise guidance at an early phase of the writing process and was gracious enough to review the final draft. Katie Eberle's love for nature and artistic eye come through in the stunning cover. Thanks to Tom Jennings for your editorial assistance, helping us separate the wheat from the chaff. Many thanks as well to Katie Sheehan and Liz McKellar for wholeheartedly helping the book find its readers.

Dozens of early readers gave us their heartfelt impressions, and their suggestions vastly improved the text. Enormous thanks to David Butler and Fiona Cheong for their incredibly detailed and helpful suggestions that touched almost every line of the book. Thanks to Sumi Loundon Kim for your last-minute advice—you were right on! Leah Naomi Green brought her poet's eye to the early sections of the book, and Arthur McKeown brought a keen eye to the book's philosophical vision.

Brother Phap Luu would like to thank Ernest Hebert for his extraordinary writing mentorship, for his comment thirty years ago ("Don't send me a manuscript unless you already have a publisher"), and for his spot-on suggestions; Barbara Will for introducing him to the most important US literature of the twentieth century and for her encouragement to make the book relevant to the crises of our time; and Melissa Zeiger for her wise mentorship thirty years ago and her comments highlighting the emotional core of the book.

Jim Collins helped us clean up the writing, and Willow Nilsen helped us make sure it would be a trustworthy and relevant guide for modern-day backpackers and nature lovers. Thanks to Orlaith O'Sullivan for her work to change the world with mindfulness, one child and one teacher at a time, and for sharing her thoughts on our book. Thanks to Bruce Nichols for sticking with us even when you were rightly dubious about this Appalachian Trail adventure run by the monks, for your wisdom, and for believing in us. Joe "forty-below Joe" Spaeder from the Homer, Alaska Sangha helped us conceptualize hiking retreats back in 2006 and provided excellent feedback on an early version of this book.

We thank all our monastic brothers and sisters for being inspired to take part in (and hopefully continue!) these crazy backpacking and walking retreats. Thank you to Brother Phap Man (Aaron Solomon), Brother Phap Khoi (Lazy Monk), Brother Phap Ly, and Brother Dao Hanh for joining us on the epic 2018 Appalachian Trail hike described in the book. You are all present on every page. Thank you to many other siblings, monastic and lay, who supported our walking and backpacking retreats in Germany, Southern California, and Nepal: Sister Tong Nghiem, Sister Huong Nghiem, Brother Phap Tri, Sister Tuyet Nghiem, Sister Bang Nghiem, Sister Chinh Nghiem, Sister Phu Nghiem, Brother Phap Lich, Sister Bien Nghiem, Sister Trang Loc Uyen, Brother Nguyen Luc, Brother Troi Ky Ngo, Sister Trang Thuy Tien, Sister Trang Thuan Hau, Sister Trang Thien Ly, Sister Trang Hai Chieu, Brother Troi Minh An, Brother Troi Minh Luong, Brother Troi Minh Niem, Brother Troi Minh Dinh, and others we may have missed. We are grateful for Fabio Cappiello's heroic work with Brother Troi Dao Phuong in developing mindful walking in Italy on the path of St. Francis. Thanks to Brother Phap Dung, Brother Phap Linh, and Sister True Dedication for their early support of the Appalachian Trail hike as a retreat.

Ramon Carreras—how can we thank you enough? You understood without hesitation that healing comes from being in nature—whether on skis or on foot. Your companionship and spiritual support have been invaluable. Bouillon?

Thank you to the entire Plum Village community for providing the time and space for us to work on this book; thank you to the Deer Park community for supporting the building of a small writing hut for us to work in. Special thanks to our elders: Brother Phap An for his ongoing support of the walking retreats at the EIAB, Brother Phap Ung for his spiritual support in Plum Village, and Brother Phap Dung for seeing the value of backpacking retreats at Deer Park.

Thank you, Sister Kaira Jewel, for pioneering the hiking retreats in Germany with the support of Ivo Scheppers and Johannes Thomm. We continue in your footsteps. Tom and Christine Vesey were kind at a crucial moment in the book's genesis, making their family house in the Pyrenees available to us. Thanks to Marc Benioff for his generous support of the Appalachian Trail hike; Jem Fredhamn (Brother Phap Ho) for his brotherhood, his abiding love of wild nature, his kind management of the bank account holding our budget, and for spearheading the Earth Holders movement; Joydeep Kamdar for getting our vision of a mobile monastery and helping us to realize it in Nepal; Hemant Soreng for his steady and wise guidance so we could realize the mobile monastery in the Himalayas; Anita Constantini for her creative and visionary approach to mindful walking retreats in nature in Italy—we hope everyone has a chance to walk with her.

Thanks to Brian "B" Wolford and Katie "Tonks" Tonkavich for being critical catalysts of the backpacking retreats at Deer Park Monastery; Joaquin Carral, and Aurora Teresa Leon Conde for believing in our vision of the Appalachian Trail hike, helping us fundraise for it, and for your sage and mindful presence.

Special thanks to Caitanya Cook, George Mangual, Severin Kodderitzsch, and Jonathan Harris for your continuing support of Path of Happiness retreats and helping to make this book become a beautiful flower. Thank you to every person who participated in a Path of Happiness or Wanderretreat. Your practice and insights have helped us to grow as practitioners.

Finally, Brother Phap Xa thanks brother Phap Luu for his brotherhood, creativity, humor, and commitment to writing this book. Brother Phap Luu wholeheartedly thanks Brother Phap Xa for suggesting the idea on that fateful day in Washington, DC and for his constant friendship, humor, and dedication.

We have been supported by countless other folks and beings not mentioned here. Please excuse us for any unintentional omission. We remain deeply grateful for your support of our path.

ABOUT THE AUTHORS

PHAP XA (pronounced "fap sah," Brother Equanimity) is a Dutch monk ordained by Zen Master Thich Nhat Hanh in 2003. He became a Dharma teacher in 2010 and has lived and practiced in Plum Village, France; Blue Cliff Monastery in upstate New York, United States; and the European Institute of Applied Buddhism (EIAB) in Germany, where he is especially known for leading several popular hiking retreats each year, both locally and overseas. Since 2015, Phap Xa has offered courses on mindful tea drinking, as tea meditation has been his daily practice for many years.

Ordained in 2003, **PHAP LUU** (pronounced "fap lu," Brother Stream) received the Transmission of the Lamp to teach the Dharma from Zen Master Thich Nhat Hanh in 2011. He helped start Wake Up, the Plum Village movement for young people, as well as the Happy Farm, Plum Village's organic farming community, and has been working with Wake Up Schools since its inception in 2012 to bring mindfulness to schools. Phap Luu has served as a monastic editor for several books by Thích Nhất Hạnh, including *Happy Teachers Change the World*, *Stepping into Freedom*, *The Admonitions and Encouraging Words of Master Guishan*, *How to Focus*, and *Cracking the Walnut*. He initiated the Buddha the Scientist retreat and symposium series and leads mindful backpacking retreats in nature around Deer Park Monastery in Southern California; Joshua Tree National Park; the Sierra Nevada; and on the Appalachian Trail.

PARALLAX PRESS, a nonprofit publisher founded by Zen Master Thich Nhat Hanh, publishes books and media on the art of mindful living and Engaged Buddhism. We are committed to offering teachings that help transform suffering and injustice. Our aspiration is to contribute to collective insight and awakening, bringing about a more joyful, healthy, and compassionate society.

View our entire library at parallax.org.

THE MINDFULNESS BELL is a journal of the art of mindful living in the Plum Village tradition of Thich Nhat Hanh. To subscribe or to see the worldwide directory of sanghas (local mindfulness groups), visit mindfulnessbell.org.

For information on upcoming Hiking Zen retreats, visit hikingzen.org.